GOOD DESIGN IS FOR EVERYONE

GOOD DESIGN IS FOR EVERYONE

THE FIRST 10 YEARS OF
PEPSICO DESIGN + INNOVATION

New York · Paris · London · Milan

AN EXTRAORDINARY
JOURNEY

When I became CEO of PepsiCo in 2018, one of the first things I did was reach out to our Chief Design Officer, Mauro Porcini. I told him that I had a special assignment for him. It wasn't about designing a new product or reimagining one of our iconic brands. It was about transforming our culture. I needed the entire Design team to think differently; to question our assumptions, to bring a designer's eye and a disruptor's mindset to a company that needed to shake things up.

By that time, Mauro had been leading our Design function since its formation in 2012. For the first six years of its existence, Design had been operating with a *start-up* mindset; as a creative group of pioneers turning out high-quality work. Now, I wanted PepsiCo to take things to the next level and become a fully design-driven company — a company aiming to be the most people-focused and innovative organization in the world. In other words, Design needed to graduate to a *scale-up* mindset. That meant the Design team needed a seat at every table, and they needed to be among the loudest voices.

This elevation of a people-first approach to innovation was directly tied to the changes we were seeing in society — changes that have only accelerated since 2018. People are demanding what they want, when they want it, at a price they can afford. They want products that are better for themselves and the planet. And they want to feel a personal connection to their favorite brands. To put it simply, the future of brand-building and product innovation, along with the future of organizational culture, is *human*.

In this book, we celebrate the many ways our Design organization has pushed the boundaries of what it means to be a human-centered company.

One way is through exciting product innovations, like SodaStream Professional. This is our custom beverage fountain that lets people create their own water experience — from flavors and functional ingredients to temperature, carbonation, and more — adopting reusable bottles and a QR code to limit single-use plastic and save their personal preferences. SodaStream Professional is a critical tool for building out our ecosystem of customized beverage options, whilst also helping to meet the needs of people who are looking to lead healthier, more sustainable lives. By centering our innovation around people, we create value for individuals and for society.

But the impact of the Design function goes well beyond products and experiences. For a decade, our designers have been at the very center of our effort to transform PepsiCo's culture by placing users, consumers, and customers first, voicing their opinions fearlessly, acting as owners, and focusing and getting work done fast. Even before these were key behaviors of The PepsiCo Way, this approach was already part of the Design team's instinct, their unique style of thinking and acting. Over the past four years, as we have embraced Winning with pep+ (PepsiCo Positive), they have done even more to place these values front and center, setting a powerful example within the company and in the world. Today PepsiCo is a company infused with design-led thinking, and through surface of the impact that the Design organization has had on PepsiCo over the past ten years. This book lays out our transformation to a more people-focused approach to innovation; a journey that has not only created growth for our company and our share-holders, but has also created untold value for our users, our consumers, our customers, our communities, and our planet.

On behalf of the entire company, I want to thank everyone who has worked on the PepsiCo Design mission over the past decade. Every single one of you has made a positive difference to the company, and the world. It has been an extraordinary journey filled with countless smiles, and I look forward to another ten years of inspirational, sustainable, human-centered design.

→ **RAMON LAGUARTA**
CHAIRMAN AND CHIEF EXECUTIVE OFFICER

JUST THE BEGINNING

When a recruiter called me in November 2011 at my home in Minneapolis, telling me that PepsiCo wanted to connect with me for the newly created role of Chief Design Officer, I told her that it was a great position, but I wasn't interested. I was already the Chief Design Officer of 3M, another American multinational corporation. I was working on exciting innovation projects, leveraging more than fifty different technology platforms, covering more than sixty industries in almost every existing product category. What more could I do at PepsiCo?

But the recruiter and PepsiCo's talent acquisition team were insistent. They persuaded me to reflect and have a chat with Brad Jakeman, President of PepsiCo's Global Beverage Group at the time, and afterward with then-CEO Indra Nooyi. I am grateful for the resilience of those recruiters. Those conversations activated a journey of discovery that brought me to fully understand the infinite opportunities that an intelligent approach to design-driven innovation could generate for any business, in any industry, in any corner of the planet. It was then I saw the role as CDO at PepsiCo for what it was: an incredible chance to share the endless potential of design and human-centricity with the world.

From 2012 to 2018, the first six years of our PepsiCo Design function, under Indra's leadership and vision, were an era of discovery, trial and error, building and testing and prototyping. I was fortunate to bring together an amazing team of creative, intelligent, empathetic people, sponsored by a visionary CEO. We approached the building of the new capability and culture from scratch, in much the same way we would approach a design project, blending the three pillars of design thinking: empathy, strategy, and prototyping.

Together with this incredible group of people and our sponsors and co-conspirators, we had some fantastic successes, from the experiences we imagined and created for Milan Design Week to our design collaborations with multiple customers in the food service industry to innovations like Pepsi Spire. One of our first global undertakings was the 2014 refresh of the Pepsi visual identity, Big Bold Blue, which unified the look of the brand worldwide for the first time. It paved the way for what now, ten years later, has become one of our most ambitious brand design projects to date: the 2023 Pepsi Global Redesign. Over the last decade, PepsiCo's Design function has evolved alongside our iconic cola brand and other global brands in our portfolio, growing bolder and more culturally relevant as our organization transforms and embraces a new vision of what we do and how we do it.

The first decade of PepsiCo Design has shown us, and the world, the power and possibility of an in-house group of pioneering creatives. However, none of this would be possible without our "co-conspirators" and sponsors. Leaders like Indra Nooyi and Ramon Laguarta have been essential for the success of this new creative culture.

In 2018, when Ramon Laguarta became CEO, his vision helped us scale new heights. And projects like SodaStream Professional, the Gatorade Gx system, the Stax paper canister, and now Pepsi's global redesign are some manifestations of that collaboration. Ramon understands what even some designers don't: that design-driven means human-centered. It means sustainable from an environmental standpoint and also from a visual, functional, intellectual, emotional, and social point of view. Design-driven means meaningful innovation for people. It's all about them. If our solutions are designed in the best way possible — in the most *human* way possible — then we will end up adding value to people's lives, generating moments of positivity made up of security, comfort, utility, convenience, pleasure, style, beauty, enjoyment, meaning, and poetry. This *effort*, consequently, will be a fundamental driver for the organization's growth. When human value meets financial value, magic happens.

So, it's up to us as designers and innovators to embrace the people — the human beings — who are at the center of our task. Over the past ten years, I am proud to say that's exactly what we've done at PepsiCo. We have found our identity in this journey; we have met friends, allies, and mentors. We have converted skeptics into extraordinary sponsors with the strength of good ideas and a good heart, empathy, generosity, intelligence, optimism, resilience, curiosity, passion, respect, and love. We have fully embraced what it means to be *people in love with people*.

And the key to all of our success, the secret ingredient, not surprisingly, is our own people. Extraordinary people, who are extraordinarily difficult to find. I call those people "unicorns." I work with unicorns every day. The PepsiCo Design organization has been a breeding ground for unicorns for a decade. Many of them are still with us; many more will join us in the future; some of them have left and gone on to do great things. Together, as you will see in this book, our work has helped place PepsiCo at the nexus of culture and creativity, of purpose and profit. And with the support of business leaders and partners spread all around the company, our influence will only continue to grow as we fully embrace our PepsiCo Positive strategy and design a better world that drives positive action for the planet and people. Because being a design-driven company is not just up to designers — it's everybody's job.

Society is entering an age of excellence; a new world in which every company will always have a greater need for design-driven innovation — an entirely humanist type of innovation with a sincere, obsessive, unavoidable attention to the needs and wants of every human being.

That is what we have tried to do at PepsiCo. We are in the middle of this journey and proud of what we have done so far. But this is just the beginning.

MAURO PORCINI
SENIOR VICE PRESIDENT AND CHIEF DESIGN OFFICER

BETWEEN THE DUNGEON AND THE PALACE

Our story begins in a dungeon and ends in a palace.

It began in 2012 when PepsiCo's then-CEO Indra Nooyi and former President of PepsiCo's Global Beverage Group Brad Jakeman brought on Mauro Porcini, the company's first-ever Chief Design Officer. Mauro's mandate was to incubate and develop a new Design capability in the corporation, infusing design thinking into PepsiCo's culture and leading a new human-centered approach to innovation, extending from physical to virtual expressions of the brands, including product, packaging, events, fashion and art collaborations, retail activations, architecture, and digital.

In his first few months, Mauro recruited a small but passionate team of creatives with a shared dream of building a Design capability that could drive positive change for the company, the industry, and the planet.

The PepsiCo headquarters in Purchase, New York is a one-hour drive from New York City. Knowing that the design community is predominantly based in the city, we were very conscious that to attract the best design talent, we needed a studio that was easily accessible to the creative talent in Manhattan and Brooklyn.

Even though we had the full support of some of our top executives, including our CEO, we decided to prove ourselves before asking for more funding to create a state-of-the-art design center in New York City. And so, we found a very affordable and cramped office in Midtown Manhattan to launch our venture. We had a start-up mindset, and that space, in its ugliness and inefficiency, was the perfect start-up environment. We lovingly started to call that office "The Dungeon." From there, we set out to demonstrate the value of Design in the company and in the world.

The Dungeon became our sanctuary, entrepreneurial temple, and creative home, and we felt excited and privileged to be there. So much so that many on our team — in part irony and part aspiration — began to call our workspace a different name: "The Palace."

During this incubation phase, we worked tirelessly to deliver proof of the value Design could generate for PepsiCo. We built our team of "co-conspirators": people at PepsiCo who championed our mission. In less than a year, we launched the new Pepsi visual identity system and the hi-tech Spire soda fountains. These two projects became game changers for us. People, not just at PepsiCo but in the design world, began to take note.

As our team grew and we took on bigger projects, we readied ourselves to move on from The Dungeon. The business case was there and was starting to become evident to anyone who encountered our new "design initiative." We started looking for a studio that would enable us to access local New York City creative talent while scaling our efficiency to new heights. After months of searching, we found a space at 350 Hudson in lower Manhattan that was raw except for its towering columns. An empty office to

some, but to us, it was a blank canvas; a space we could make our own, where we could build the "new" palace we dreamed of.

In September 2013, the Design Center's doors opened in New York City. Established explicitly for co-creation, people across PepsiCo came to the Design Center to collaborate with our teams and see what our culture was about. We began engaging customers, content creators, and thought leaders in cross-disciplinary conversations, many of whom have shaped our business trajectory.

Still, we knew that to deliver on Design's promise, it couldn't just exist in an ivory tower. Our team needed to be as global as our portfolio and the people whose lives our brands touch daily. In 2014 we opened our first global Design Center in Shanghai, China. Within a few months it became a massive success, marking the beginning of our "glocal" approach that generates outstanding design work by infusing our global strategy with our design leaders' cultural perspectives and on-the-ground knowledge of their local communities. Our success in China was the first of many. Next were offices in Chicago, Illinois, and in Plano, Texas. And then London, Mexico City, and Moscow. What started in the dungeon spread across the globe. And in 2015, we doubled our office space in Manhattan and took over an entire floor at 350 Hudson.

In 2018, Ramon Laguarta became the new CEO of PepsiCo. A longtime partner of our Design organization while he was leading the European business, Ramon always understood the value and potential of Design. Within his first year of leadership, our team doubled in size. We incubated even newer capabilities and embraced a scale-up mindset to take PepsiCo to the next level, making it faster, stronger, and better. Together we built our design teams in Ireland, Brazil, India, Egypt, Thailand, and most recently, South Africa and Turkey, with more to come in the future. As a company, we embraced pep+ (PepsiCo Positive), a bold new agenda to drive positive action for the planet and its people.

Between The Dungeon and our "new" Palace, we propelled the growth of our multidisciplinary global team to over 300 creatives united in harnessing the power of design for positive change. Since its inception, our team has been honored with over 1,800 design and innovation awards, has driven efficiency for PepsiCo, and has generated many new revenue streams for our global food and beverage portfolio.

But since the beginning, we've always been inspired by one shared value: our love for people. The first ten years of PepsiCo Design have shown us that the palace exists wherever we come together to create real value for people and our planet. And when you have that kind of purpose, it doesn't matter where your story begins. The important thing is that there is no end.

1898–1904

1905–1949

1950–1986

1987–1997

1998–2007

2008–2022

PEPSI
ZERO SUGAR
WILD CHERRY
FLAVOR WITH OTHER NATURAL FLAVORS

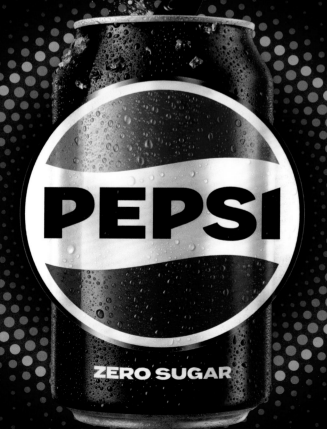

PEPSI 2012 GLOBAL
BIG BOLD BLUE

→ A decade before the new Pepsi visual identity
is unveiled, this refresh unifies Pepsi worldwide
for the first time.

140 YEARS OF QUAKER OATS

(2017) UNITED STATES

→ Our limited edition cannister celebrates
140 years of craftsmanship and authenticity.

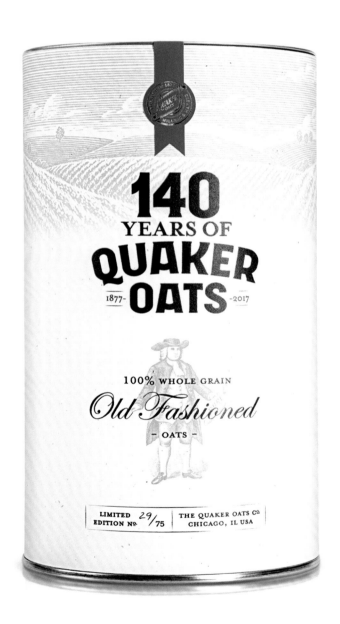

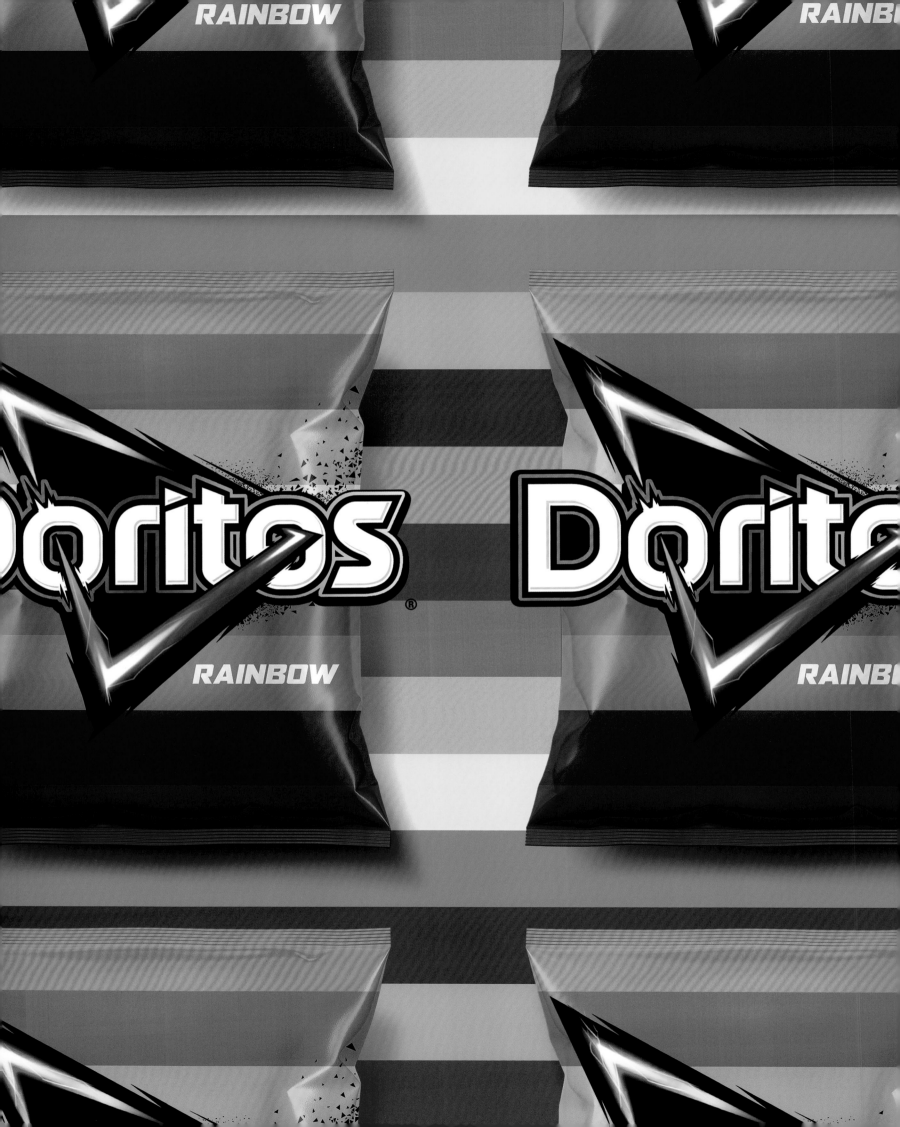

DORITOS
RAINBOW
BRAZIL (2021) BRAZIL

→ We drew inspiration from the symbolic pride flag
to illustrate our love and demonstrate the power of
color to make a statement.

DORITOS
RAINBOW
BRAZIL

(2022) BRAZIL

→ For Brazil Pride, showstopping color and
bold typography celebrate how we're all
as unique as our fingerprints.

SODASTREAM
PROFESSIONAL

(2020) GLOBAL

→ Our modern hydration platform seamlessly
integrates into any space to enable personalized
and sustainable hydration at work or on the go.

SODASTREAM PROFESSIONAL USER INTERFACE

(2020) GLOBAL

→ A connected and circular ecosystem allows you to customize and save your water's flavor, temperature, and carbonation level while automatically tracking your unique hydration and sustainability goals.

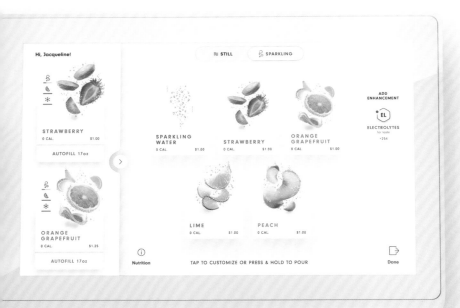

56%

HYDRATION GOAL

You're on the way to hitting
your daily goal of 64oz.

120

BOTTLES SAVED

120 16-oz plastic bottles
saved at this station

1oz

PAUSE

PEPSI ✕
PEACEBIRD (2016—2017) CHINA

→ Vintage Pepsi iconography takes our classic
collection from the street to the runway.

PEACEBIRD

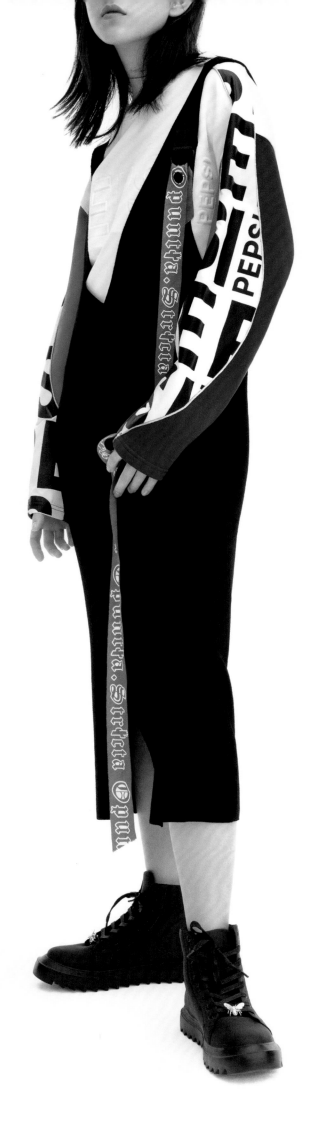

CHEETOS 2019 BRAZIL
MANSION

→ Step inside Chester Cheetah's delicious dream house
for Cheetos-infused food and fun.

PEPSI
✕ LUSON (2022) CHINA

→ Strength and style combine to create
a winning collection worthy of a spot in
every Pepsi lover's closet.

R&D AND DESIGN
ARE FORMIDABLE PARTNERS.
TOGETHER THEY RESEARCH,
DISCOVER, AND CREATE THE
FUTURE OF PEPSICO.

WE'RE EXCITED TO CONTINUE
TO SEE HOW DESIGN-LED
INNOVATION,
TECHNOLOGY, AND SCIENCE CAN
COMPLEMENT ONE ANOTHER
AND EVOLVE OUR PORTFOLIO TO
DELIVER PEPSICO-POSITIVE
TRANSFORMATION.

RENÉ LAMMERS
→ EXECUTIVE VICE PRESIDENT AND CHIEF SCIENCE OFFICER

QUAKER
OATS REBRAND

(2018) UNITED STATES

→ The values at the heart of this iconic brand
anchor a refresh of the nutrition favorite.

QUAKER
~ ESTᴰ 1877 ~
™

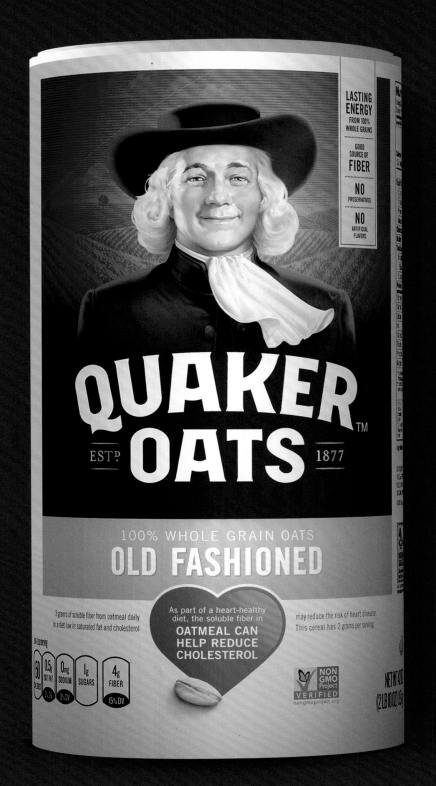

LAY'S
SIGNATURE✕LABELHOOD

(2019) CHINA

→ Our immersive pop-up redefines the Lay's experience by inviting people to express themselves through flavors crafted just for them.

LAY'S
SIGNATURE✕LANE
CRAWFORD

(2020) CHINA

→ Personalized chips steal the show at a tasty, must-share event.

LAY'S
SIGNATURE
WINTER
HOLIDAY
MARKET

→ In Shanghai, couples tell their love stories with this sweet experience offering indulgent and personalized flavors.

SMART
Gx BOTTLE

(2022) UNITED STATES

→ The LED cap lights on this tech-enabled squeeze bottle indicate your progress toward your daily hydration goals, which are also trackable on the Gx App.

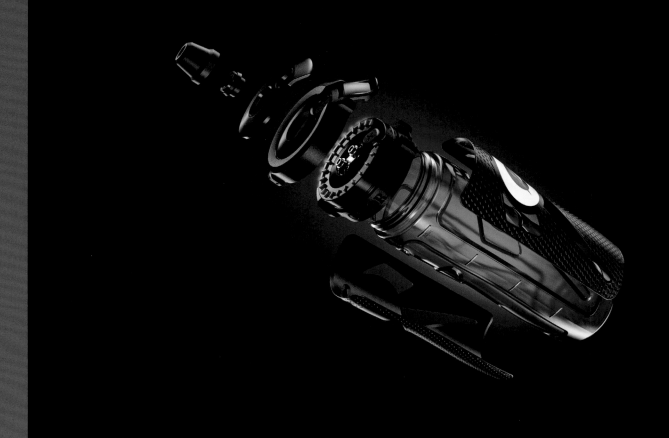

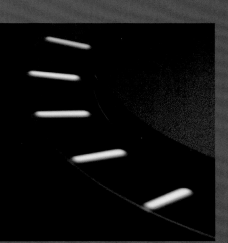

7UP ⟨2023⟩ GLOBAL
GLOBAL BRAND RESTAGE

→ A bold new identity captures the uplifting taste and spirit
of our lemon-lime soda's feel-good vibes.

REFRESHING LEMON & LIME TASTE
7up
REFRESHING LEMON & LIME TASTE
喜

DESIGNERS PAINT THE BRANDS THAT SURROUND PEOPLE'S DAILY LIVES.

SERENA WILLIAMS

× **Gx** (2020) **UNITED STATES**

→ The limited edition Gatorade Gx Bottle we co-created with Serena Williams celebrates every type of strength.

FUN CHINA ✕
PEPSI (2020) CHINA

→ Our fashion-forward collaboration
with the culture-inspired brand serves
up an exciting streetwear drop.

SODASTREAM✕BUBLYDROPS

(2020) GLOBAL

→ The refreshing flavors of bubly and the innovative technology of SodaStream create a 360° sparkling water experience whose fun and vibrant visual system celebrates the future of sustainable, do-it-yourself hydration.

MTN DEW
ALL-STAR WEEKEND
COURTSIDE STUDIO

(2020) **UNITED STATES**

→ Our experience in the heart of Chicago's
West Loop gives basketball fans
unprecedented access to their favorite
sports stars and culture makers.

BIG STRAW

→ A bold redesign reimagines this snack with exuberant pop art packaging and a playful color palette reminiscent of classic comic book illustrations.

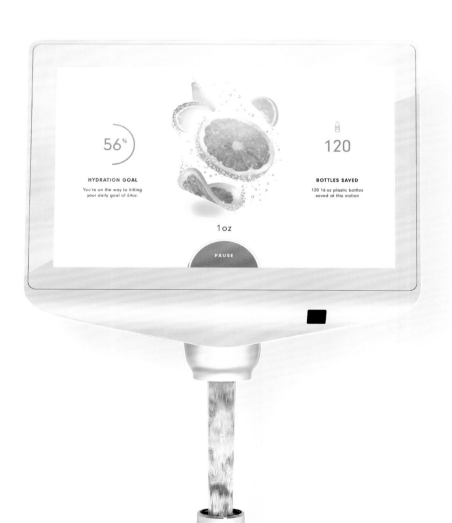

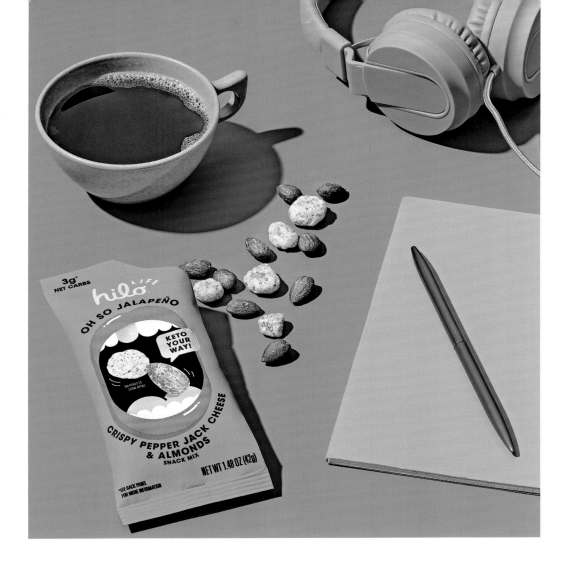

PEPSI
CULTURE SERIES—
MEXICO

(2020) MEXICO

→ Our limited edition Pepsi cans proudly
express local pride by highlighting
the traditions and unique flavors of six
iconic cities in Mexico.

MĒRIDA

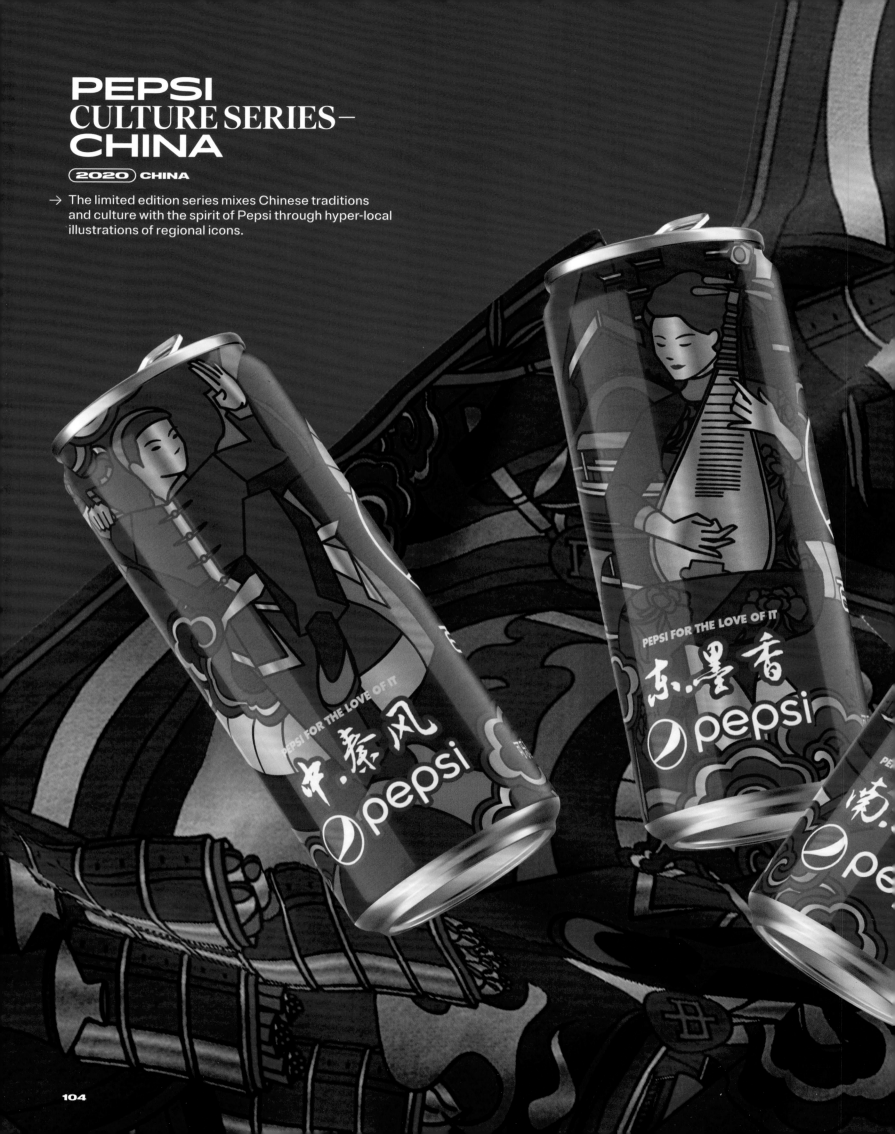

PEPSI CULTURE SERIES— CHINA

(2020) CHINA

→ The limited edition series mixes Chinese traditions and culture with the spirit of Pepsi through hyper-local illustrations of regional icons.

PEPSI
CULTURE SERIES—
KUWAIT

(2020) KUWAIT

→ A montage of traditional folk instruments, skyline silhouettes, and crafted teapots captures the rich culture of this country on the Persian Gulf.

PEPSI CULTURE SERIES— JORDAN

(2020) JORDAN

→ Textile patterning and sophisticated illustrations of the rock city of Petra, the Roman Theater, and musical instruments celebrate the vibrant heritage of Jordan.

PEPSI × PUMA

2019 GLOBAL

→ Two iconic brands combine to celebrate the next generation of style for the 50th anniversary of the iconic suede shoe.

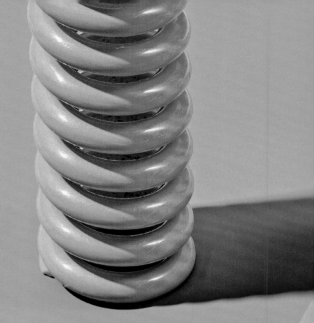

HILO LIFE

→ A bright identity upends expectations to introduce this design-led brand's joyful, keto-conscious bites.

3g* NET CARBS

12g* PROTEIN

hilo LIFE

SUPER CHEESY

KETO YOUR WAY!

ENLARGED TO SHOW DETAIL

CRISPY CHEDDAR CHEESE & ALMONDS SNACK MIX

NET WT 1.48 OZ

*SEE BACK PANEL FOR MORE INFORMATION

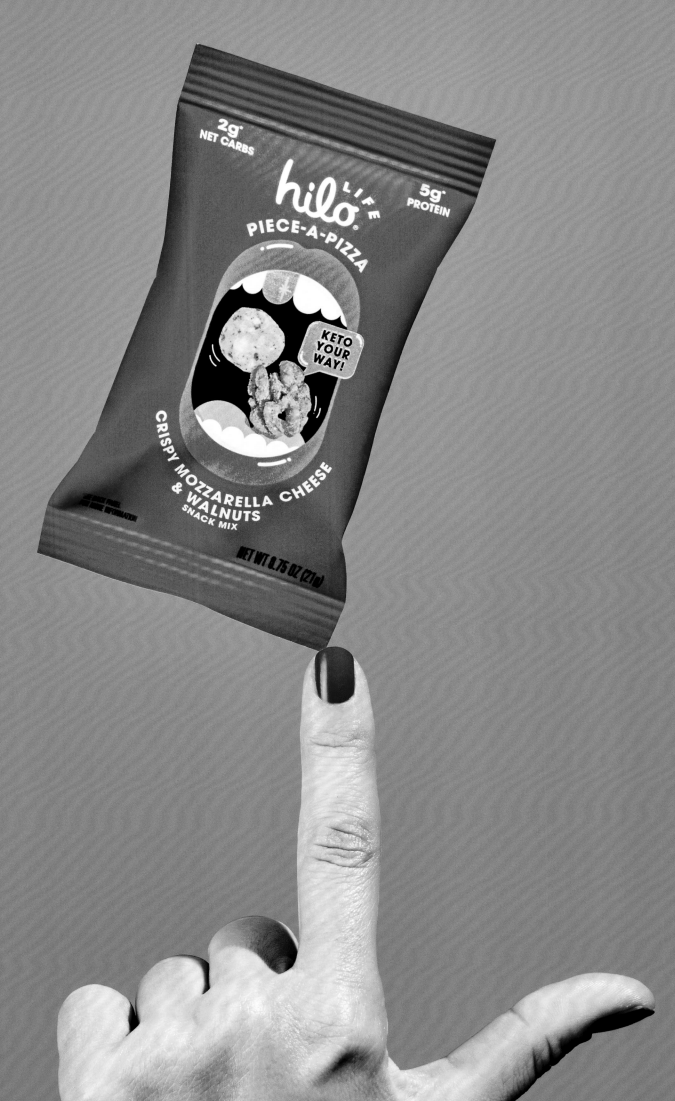

DESIGN IS AN
UNPARALLELED DRIVER OF
TOP-LINE AND BOTTOM-LINE
PERFORMANCE.

IT CAN LEAD BOTH
DIMENSIONS BECAUSE IT
BUILDS MEANINGFUL
SOLUTIONS
FOR PEOPLE, WHICH YIELDS
AN INHERENT
FINANCIAL VALUE FOR
THE COMPANY.

HUGH F. JOHNSTON
→ VICE CHAIRMAN AND CHIEF FINANCIAL OFFICER

NITRO PEPSI

(2021) UNITED STATES

→ To introduce the first-ever nitrogen-infused cola, we created a specialty glass and an expressive identity to evoke the cascade of tiny bubbles and frothy foam of this smooth, creamy, and delicious cola.

NITRO
PEPSI BAR

(2022) UNITED STATES

→ The immersive tasting experience filled with modern
mixological moments, rich blues, vanilla tones, and
copper accents brings Nitro Pepsi to life inside
the High Roller® Observation Wheel at The LINQ®
Hotel + Experience, Las Vegas.

PEPSI✕
OCTOPUS  2021 ITALY

→ The summer streetwear capsule of limited edition styles integrates the iconic colors and shapes of Pepsi with the illustrative tentacles of Octopus.

pepsi.

FOR THE LOVE OF IT

PEPSI SPIRE
PLATFORM & DIGITAL EQUIPMENT

(2013) GLOBAL

→ Our elevated Spire platform offers a modern suite of interactive beverage fountains, coolers, and ready-to-drink equipment.

SPIRE (2013) GLOBAL
USER INTERFACE

→ The beverage fountain invites fans to call the shots
and choose their own taste adventures.

CHOOSE A DRINK

pepsi

TRY UP TO 3 FLAVORS

CHERRY
VANILLA
STRAWBERRY
LEMON

POUR

ALL DRINKS

PEPSI SPIRE DESTINATION

→ Fabio Novembre offers an atmospheric experience through two bold Pepsi Spire fountain destinations inside our "Mix It Up" space.

As part of a PepsiCo exhibit during Milan Design Week, the biggest annual design event in the world, we commissioned a group of design visionaries to reinterpret people's experiences with a series of our iconic brands.

PEPSI
LICENSING
STYLE GUIDE

(2020) **UNITED STATES**

→ Our go-to resource gives our licensing partners a cohesive guidebook to ignite cultural relevance through covet-worthy products and experiences.

INNOVATION IS AN **ACT** OF **LOVE.**

PEPSI ×
NANA JUDY

2021 **UNITED STATES / AUSTRALIA**

→ Our premium streetwear range with Nana Judy
turns vintage Pepsi iconography into a modern
cola-inspired collection.

DRINKFINITY
PORTABLE
HYDRATION
SYSTEM

(2016) GLOBAL

→ The all-encompassing hydration innovation delivers a fresh pop of flavor and function with a reusable bottle and corresponding pods that empower people to transform their water into an enhanced beverage.

DRINKFINITY
BRAND&
BOTTLE
EVOLUTION

(2019) **GLOBAL**

→ Designed to be an all-in-one hydration solution,
the new Drinkfinity combines a stainless steel,
reusable bottle with a range of functional flavor pods.

POMEGRANATE
ACAI
CAFFEINE
20 CALORIES

DRINKFINITY

DRINKFINITY

DRINKFINITY

DRINKFINITY

D∞® DRINKFINITY®
WATERMELON LEMONADE
ELECTROLYTES

D∞®
WATERMELON LEMONADE
ELECTROLYTES
40 CALORIES

D∞® DRINKFINITY®
MANGO CHIA
VITAMINS

D∞® MANGO CHIA
VITAMINS
35 CALORIES

PEPSI SPIRE
LOUNGE

(2015) GLOBAL

→ The immersive space by Stefano Giovannoni takes experiential design to the next level to highlight the Pepsi Spire fountain.

As part of a PepsiCo exhibit during Milan Design Week, the biggest annual design event in the world, we commissioned a group of design visionaries to reinterpret people's experiences with a series of our iconic brands.

IMAG!NE

→ We infused creativity into each of this brand's touchpoints to craft a whimsical experience that lets your imagination soar.

Imagine what this box could be:

It's not a box, it's an art project! Cut shapes from the printed guides to create models your family can build and decorate. Please share your work with us on Instagram.

@ @imaginesnacks

Imagine what this box could be:

It's not a box, it's an art project! Cut shapes from the printed guides to create models your family can build and decorate. Please share your work with us on Instagram.

@ @imaginesnacks

151

STRANGER THINGS (2022) MEXICO
LIMITED EDITION

→ Our team in Mexico drew on the show's '80s setting to create these limited edition packs outfitted in retro-inspired logos.

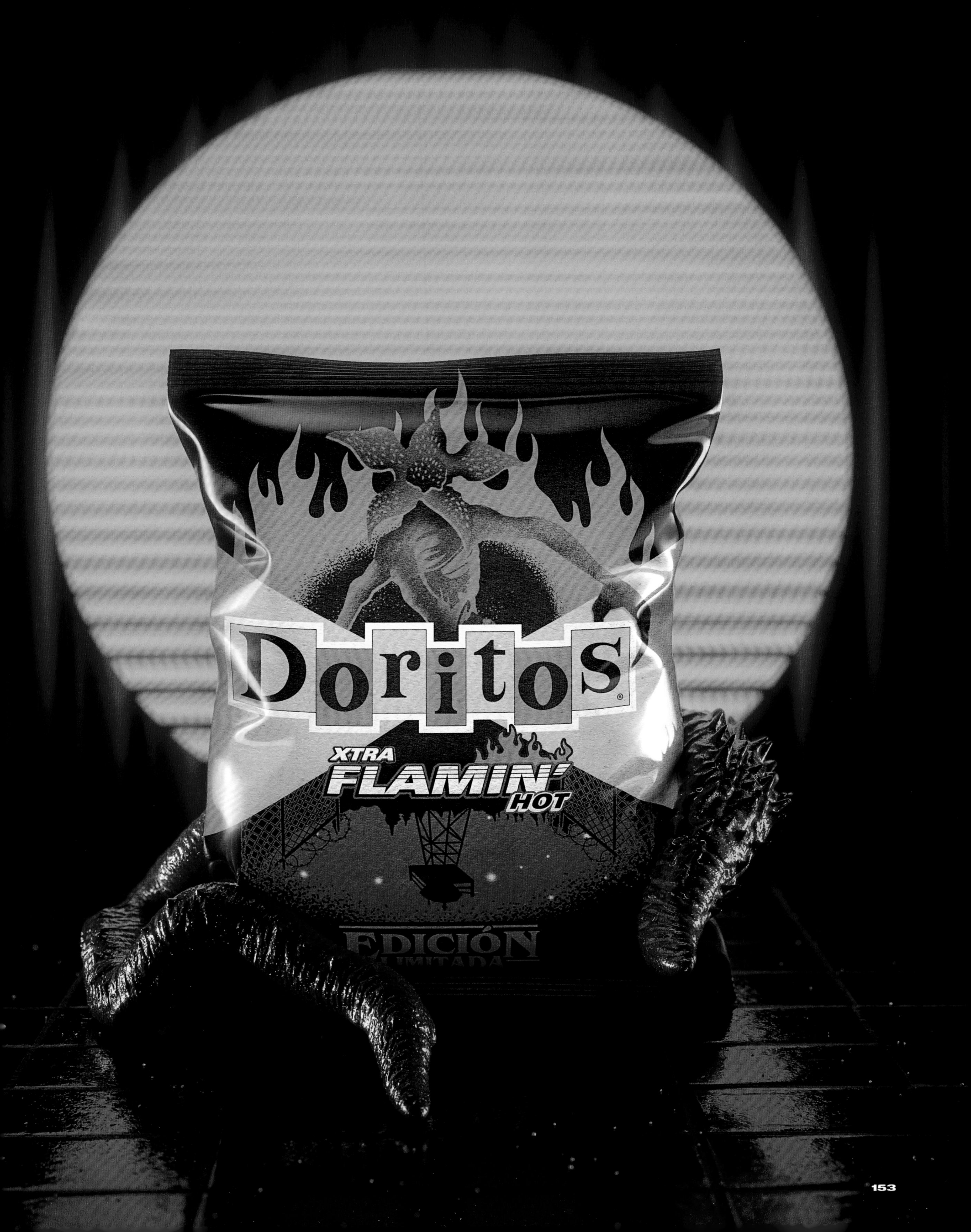
Doritos
XTRA
FLAMIN'
HOT
EDICIÓN

Gx FUEL TOMORROW COLLECTION

→ By teaming up with some of the biggest names in sports to co-create custom Gx Bottles, we are inspiring the athletes of tomorrow.

THE POWER OF ONE

LIFT UP
THE NEXT

Nothing is more important to Argentinians than community and futbol. It's a big part of our lives. If we're not rooting the best ourselves, we're cheering for our favorite team. And choosing that passion is ingrained in our culture, and we always want to share those moments with friends and family.

In Argentina, poverty prevents a lot of kids from participating in all kinds of activities. When you have a passion for community, it's unacceptable for kids to be left out. That's why my foundation addresses health, sports and education. So kids can participate in community and sports and have the chance to pursue their passions even if it's not futbol.

I'm looking today to building community and uplifting the next generation. How will you lift someone?

LIONEL MESSI
Forward
Argentina National Football Team
Paris Saint-Germain F.C.

PEPSICO NSPIRE™

(2015) GLOBAL

→ Designed by Karim Rashid, our custom innovation kitchen debuted at Milan Design Week before refreshing music and sports fans across the U.S. with gourmet snacks and customizable beverages made using our Pepsi Spire Fountain.

As part of a PepsiCo exhibit during Milan Design Week, the biggest annual design event in the world, we commissioned a group of design visionaries to reinterpret people's experiences with a series of our iconic brands.

PURPOSEFUL CREATIVITY CAN **CHANGE** THE WORLD FOR **GOOD.**

DORITOS
SOLID BLACK

(2022) **UNITED STATES**

→ Mz. Icar, an anonymous interdisciplinary arts collective composed primarily of Black women, designed fluorescent-colored bags to support Doritos SOLID BLACK, an ongoing initiative providing Black Changemakers with resources and a platform.

PEPSI ✕ EINTRACHT
LIMITED EDITION (2022) WEST EUROPE

→ A distinct and disruptive identity brings two icons together to celebrate people's love of the game and the city.

EINTRACHT
FRANKFURT
EINTRACHT
FRANKFURT
EINTRACHT
FRANKFURT
pepsi
MAX

GATORADE
BOLT PAVILION AT EXPO 2020 DUBAI

(2021) GLOBAL

→ Our lightning bolt-shaped activation invites people to zigzag through an interactive on-site experience to learn how Gatorade is fueling the next generation of athletes.

AQUAFINA
DROP PAVILION
AT EXPO 2020 DUBAI

(2021) GLOBAL

→ Crafted from 41,000 recyclable aluminum cans to look like a giant droplet, The Drop features Aquafina Water Stations to offer visitors a sustainable hydration solution and inspire action by showcasing how we can create positive change for people and the planet.

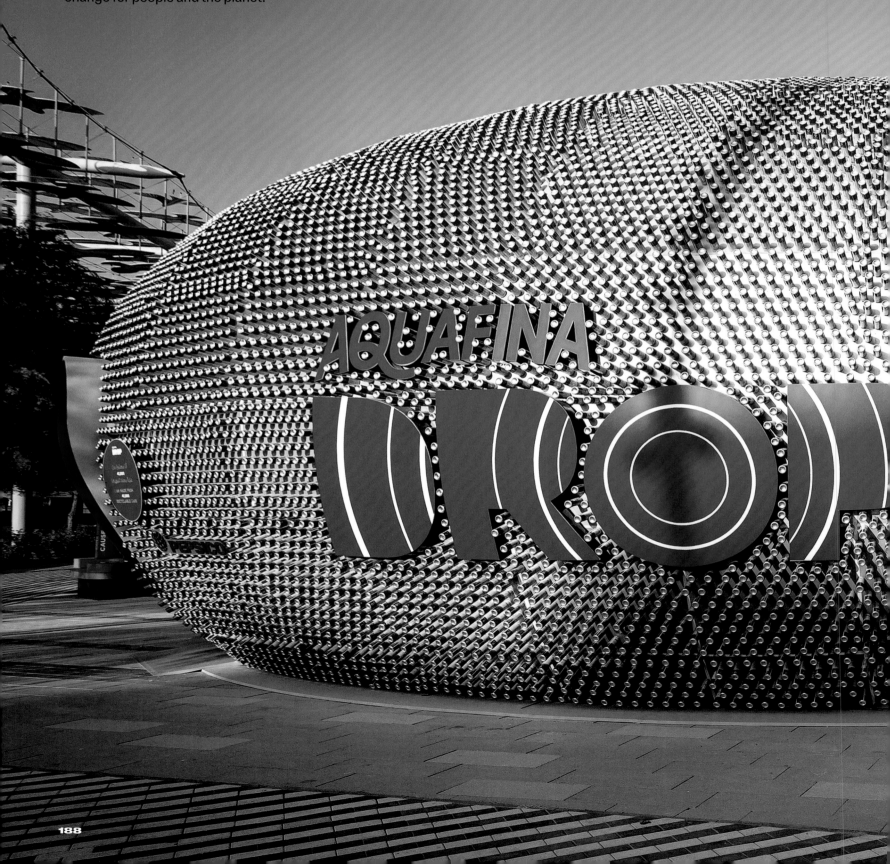

LAY'S PLUS PAVILION AT EXPO 2020 DUBAI

2021 GLOBAL

→ The Plus Pavilion blends video, scent, and sound to create an immersive and mesmerizing Lay's experience.

Experience the endless, irresistible joyful world of Lay's

LET'S GET STARTED

Experience the passion and excitement for the Beautiful Game

Lay's   Lay's   Lay's

LOCAL GROUND MATERIAL

PURE LEAF
LOUNGE

(2017) **GLOBAL**

→ Our glowing collaboration with designer Luca Nichetto offers tea lovers a refreshing oasis.

As part of a PepsiCo exhibit during Milan Design Week, the biggest annual design event in the world, we commissioned a group of design visionaries to reinterpret people's experiences with a series of our iconic brands.

PEPSI AT
METLIFE STADIUM

→ A graphic Pepsi installation kicks off the
Big Game with a big entrance.

PEPSI GATE

pepsi.

LAY'S & DORITOS OKINAWA LIMITED EDITION

(2020) CHINA

→ On-trend soy sauce and wasabi flavors inspired by Okinawa, an island in Japan, lead to wave-patterned packs decorated with hibiscus flowers and the Shisa, a symbol of protection in Okinawan mythology.

Lay's

期間限定

台湾
沖縄

柑橘醤油
シークワーサー
醤油味

PEPSI BLUE
FOR THE LOVE OF IT

(2019) UNITED STATES

→ We went all in to create a love letter and
rallying cry inspired by the pop and fizz of
our iconic brand.

DORITOS
TWISTED LIME

(2021) UNITED STATES

→ A spooky limited edition Halloween pack shaped like a pyramid invites people to join the secret society of the triangle.

DORITOS
TANGY PICKLE

(2021) UNITED STATES

→ The relaunch of a fan-favorite flavor offers serious '90s vibes with an electric visual language that extends to a wireless boombox.

PEPSI×
MONEY HEIST
LIMITED EDITION
(2021) INDIA
→ Bold and iconic designs honor the show's final season with cans that are as good as gold.

EMBRACING OUR PEP+
STRATEGY MEANS
EMBRACING INNOVATION
FOCUSED ON PEOPLE.

AS WE TRANSFORM OUR
COMPANY TO MEET THE
CHALLENGES OF THE FUTURE,
WE ARE PLACING PEOPLE
AT THE CENTER
OF OUR EFFORT TO CREATE
SUSTAINABLE GROWTH
AND INCLUSIVE VALUE, AND
DESIGN WILL CONTINUE
TO BE A CRITICAL DRIVER
OF OUR SUCCESS.

RAMON LAGUARTA
→ CHAIRMAN AND CHIEF EXECUTIVE OFFICER

DORITOS
MUSIC ALIVE
(2019) **MEXICO**

→ Music has long been a platform of the Doritos brand, and this digitally inspired collection complements our virtual concert series to celebrate bold expression.

RUFFLES
ARMORED UP
(2021) **UNITED STATES**

→ These legendary medieval-inspired kicks developed in collaboration with THE SHOE SURGEON summon you to suit up and Own Your Ridges.

GATORADE
ORGANIC

(2016) **UNITED STATES**

→ Healthy hydration wins whenever this colorful
lineup of organic flavors is spotted in the locker
room and on the sidelines.

SMARTFOOD
VALENTINE'S DAY (2022) UNITED STATES

→ We teamed up with GLAAD and queer artist Ari Liloan to create
this special pack supporting the LGBTQ+ community and celebrating
Valentine's Day in all its colors.

PEPSI × LALABOBO ⬭2017⬭ CHINA

→ Our co-branded collection with the trend-forward
fashion retailer features t-shirts, sweatshirts, dresses,
and accessories inspired by our favorite cola.

LAY'S
SAKURA

(2019) CHINA

→ Cherry blossoms infuse a much-anticipated
flavor from the inside out.

Lay's 樂事

粉櫻牛奶

Milky Sakura

每30克
能量
679千焦
(162千卡)
8%NRV
NRV(營養素參考值)

QUAKER
SMART CALORIES

(2020) CHINA

→ The nutritious solution's modern, elevated look signals the benefits of the ingredients inside.

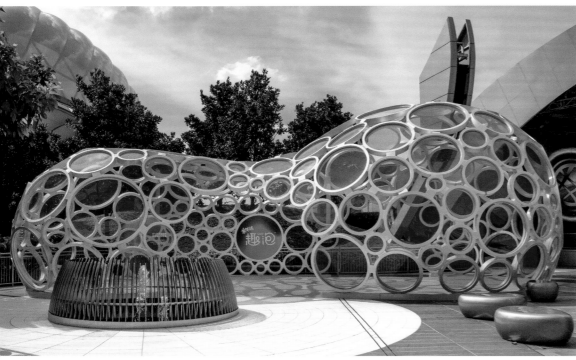

CHINESE
NEW YEAR

→ A limited edition celebration of Chinese
pride, culture, and creativity welcomes
the Year of the Ox.

YACHAK

(2021) UNITED STATES

→ For the U.S. redesign of Yachak, a bright palette, playful, nature-inspired type, and a pack of electrifying animal avatars create a high-vibe look.

MIRINDA
VISUAL IDENTITY

(2020) GLOBAL

→ Fun and flavor combine to take our fruit-flavored
carbonated soft drink brand to the next level with
an expressive, illustrated world.

CHESTER
CHEETAH
HARMONIZATION

→ When the world's only spokescheetah steps out with a fierce
new makeover, Cheetos enthusiasts bring the love.

PEPSI × PEEPS

(2021) UNITED STATES

→ Our favorite cola and the iconic springtime
treat debut a new marshmallow–flavored
cola whose vibrant, limited edition mini cans
feature sweet illustrations.

MIRINDA
GLOBAL
BRAND RESTAGE

(2023) **GLOBAL**

→ A bold "M" anchors a canvas of zesty fruit illustrations and vibrant colors to create a flavorful new identity that pops.

MIRINDA
CITRUS
DELICIOUS & FLAVOURFUL TASTE
美年达
葡萄味
DELICIOUS & FLAVOURFUL TASTE

THINKING BIG IS INCREDIBLY IMPORTANT—IT DRIVES YOU TO **CHANGE** THE **GAME** AND GIVES YOU THE ENERGY AND OPTIMISM NECESSARY TO MAKE IT HAPPEN.

ALL NEW
1893
FROM THE MAKERS OF
Pepsi-Cola

1893
FROM THE MAKERS OF
Pepsi-Cola

BLACK CURRANT
COLA
FLAVOR WITH OTHER NATURAL FLAVORS

Premium cola infused
with a bold berry finish

FAIR TRADE
CERTIFIED
SUGAR

1893
FROM THE MAKERS OF
Pepsi-Cola

CITRUS COLA
FLAVOR WITH OTHER NATURAL FLAVORS

Premium cola infused
with grapefruit essence

FAIR TRADE
CERTIFIED
SUGAR

1893

→ An unexpectedly bold cola honors our heritage and celebrates our future with vintage-inspired cans marking over 100 years of cola-making.

LAY'S
POTATO VODKA

In partnership with Portland, Oregon's Eastside Distilling, we shook things up with 1,300 individually numbered bottles of craft potato alcohol whose foiled and embossed label needs no introduction.

BRISK ZERO
DROP KIT

→ Epic new flavor launches demand even more epic influencer kits, so we created a one-of-a-kind shadowbox showcasing kicks customized by the streetwear artist, Mache.

PEPSI×FILA

(2017) SOUTH KOREA

→ The summer collaboration taps into the season with classic cola-inspired looks.

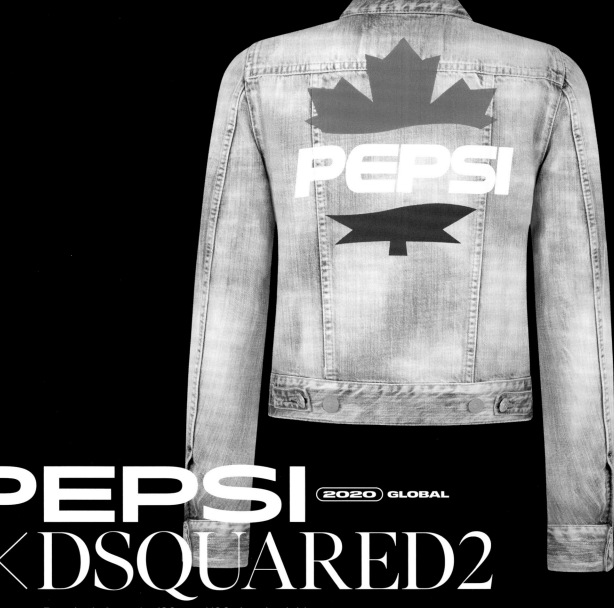

PEPSI (2020) GLOBAL
✕DSQUARED2

→ Pepsi ads from the '80s and '90s inspired this streetwear
range that brings Pepsi's classic vintage logo together with
the fashion brand's maple leaf emblem.

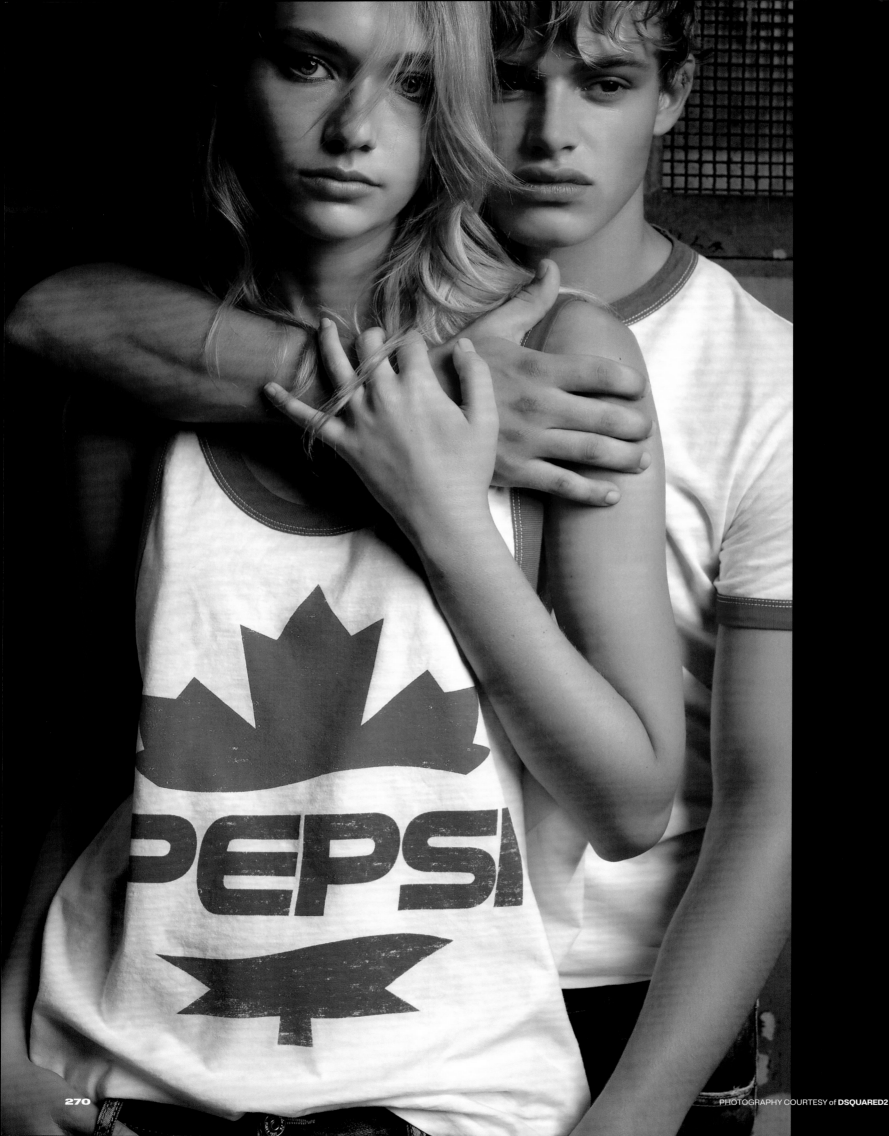

GATORADE BRAND CENTER

(2020) CHINA

→ For sports fans seeking a performance-fueled hydration experience, a stylized locker room is a win-win.

G 补给站 FUEL STATION

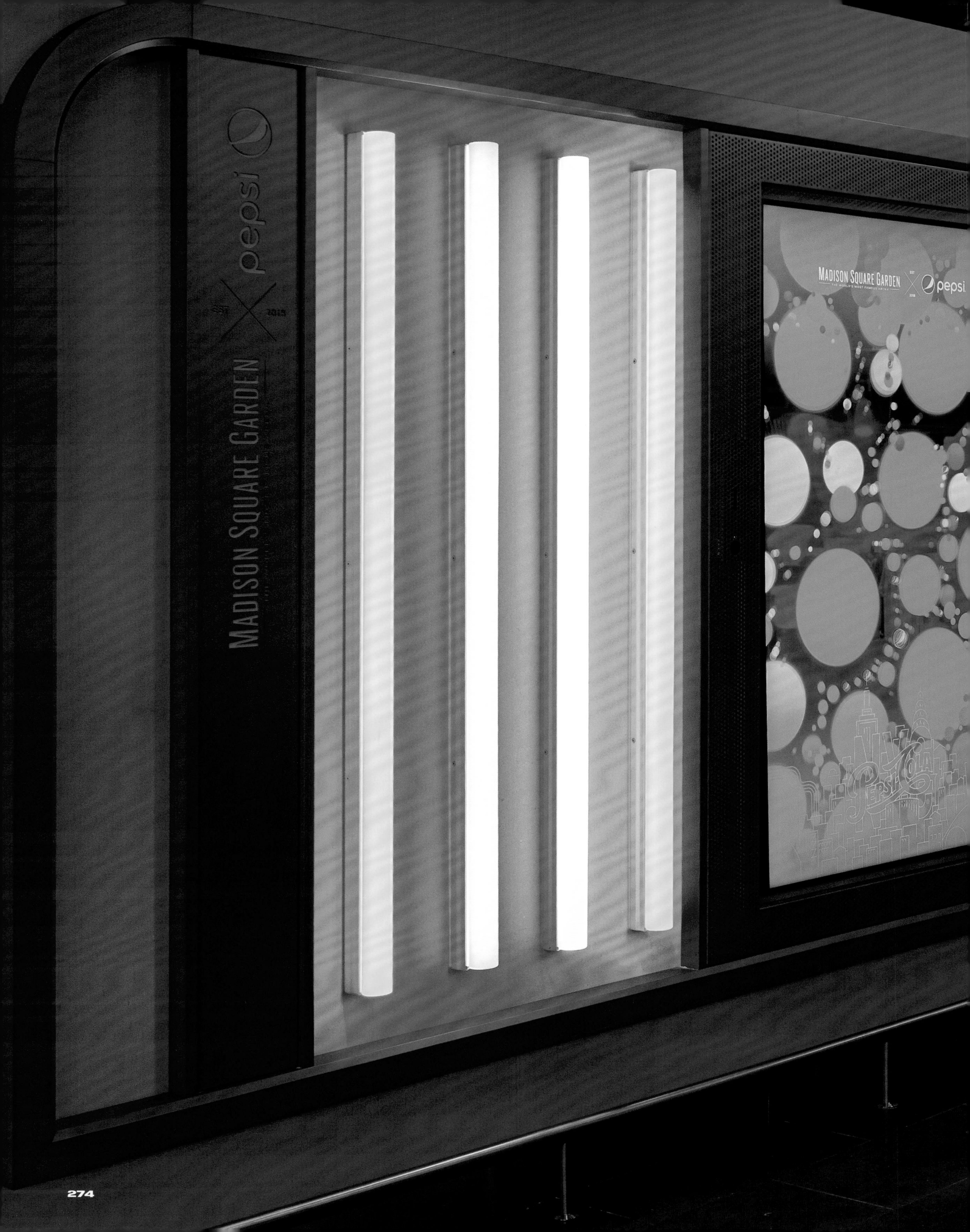
pepsi
MADISON SQUARE GARDEN
MADISON SQUARE GARDEN
pepsi

PEPSI
FAN BASE AT MADISON SQ GARDEN

(2021) **UNITED STATES**

→ Game day or showtime, the best seat in the house is one where you can enjoy an immersive celebration of your favorite cola.

WE ARE "GLOCAL"
GLOBALLY STRATEGIC AND LOCALLY RELEVANT.

PEPSI
PRESTIGE BOTTLE

(2015) GLOBAL

→ We teamed up with designer Karim Rashid to drop a modern spin on refreshment with an iconic aluminum bottle.

As part of a PepsiCo exhibit during Milan Design Week, the biggest annual design event in the world, we commissioned a group of design visionaries to reinterpret people's experiences with a series of our iconic brands.

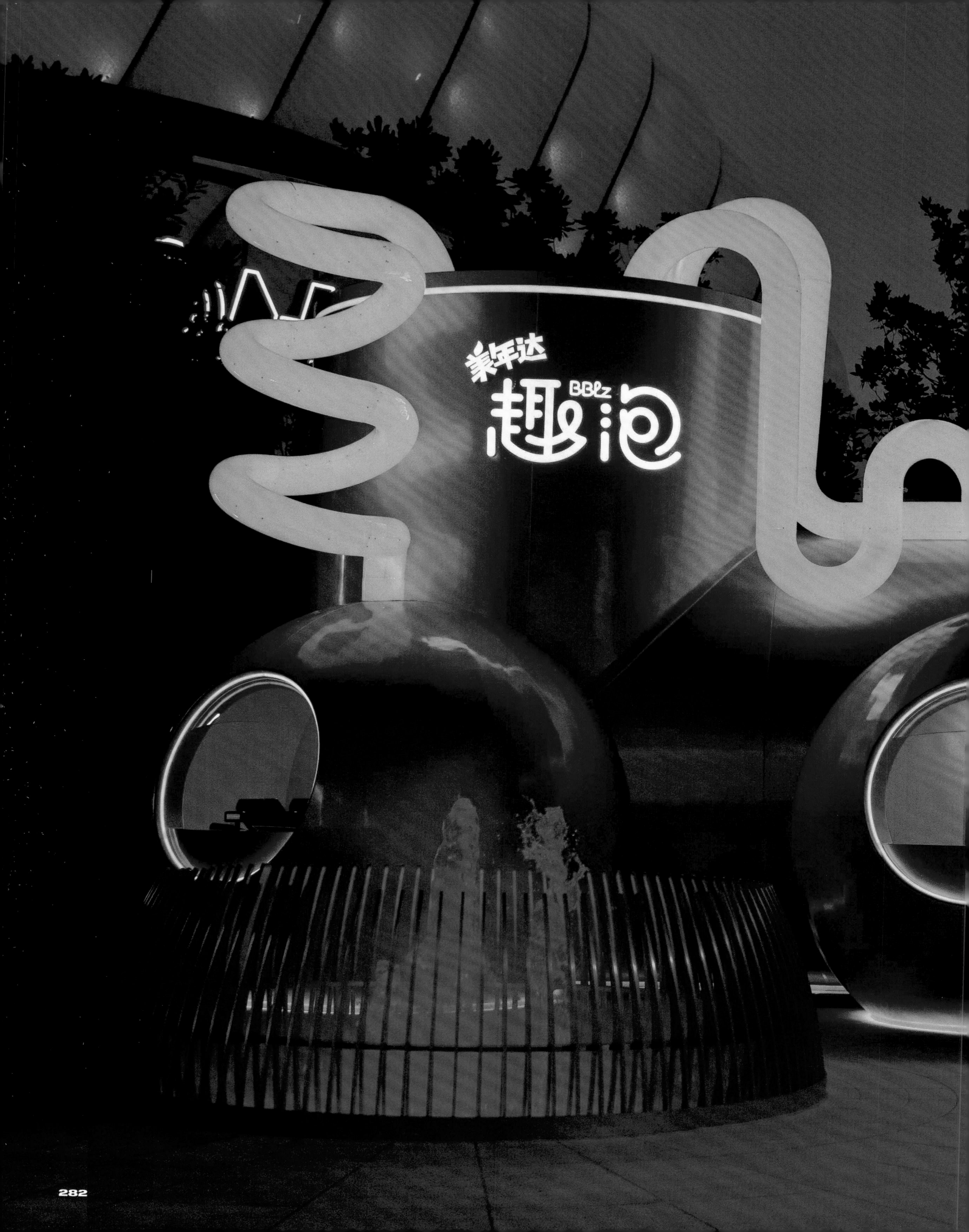
美年达
BBlz
趣泡

MIRINDA BBLZ
FUNNY LAB
SHANGHAI

→ Our multisensory summer pavilion serves up adventurous soda mixology in a colorful laboratory that's magical both day and night.

MIRINDA BBLZ
MAGIC RAINBOW
SHANGHAI

(2020) CHINA

→ The light-as-air curved dome of the Mirinda
BBLZ pavilion captures the brand's sparkling
identity and colorful, playful essence.

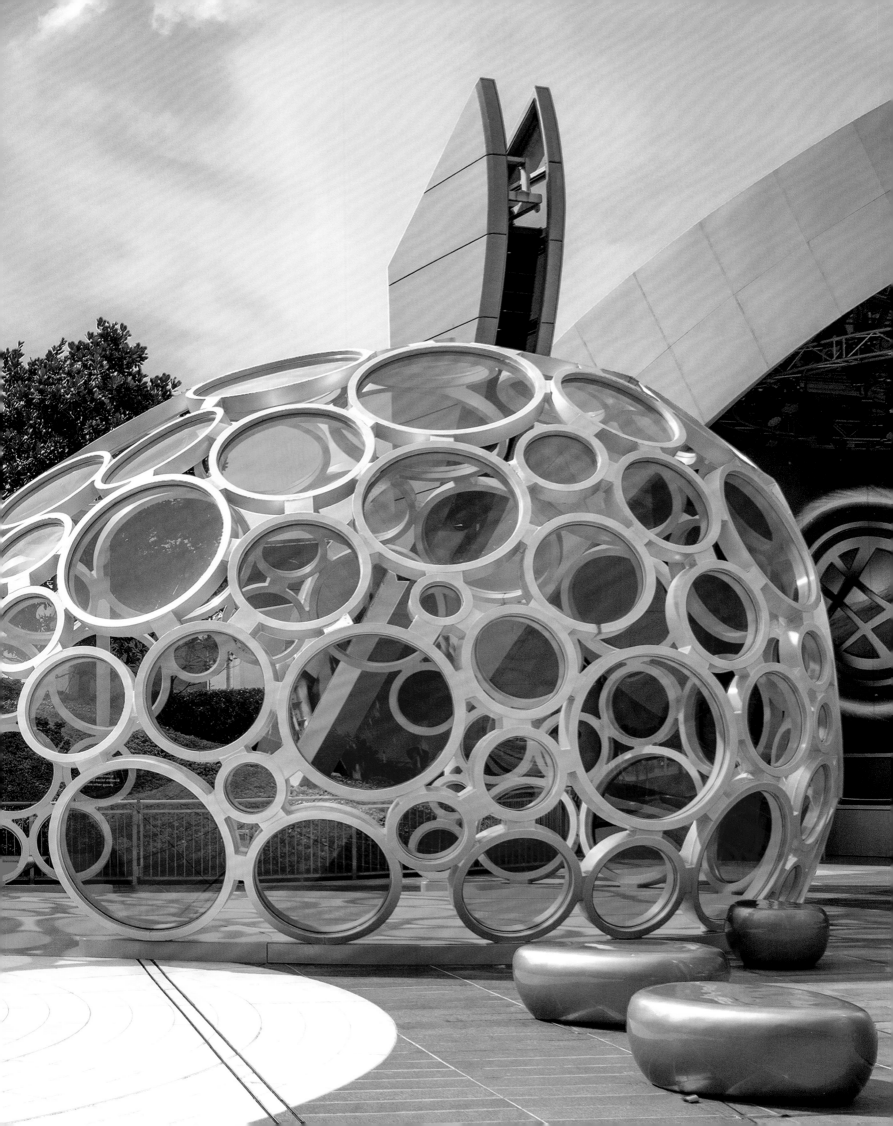

HELLO GOODNESS™ MARKETPLACE

→ Our elevated, curated marketplace brings our better-for-you brand to life through a modern experience stocked with on-the-go snacks and beverages.

7UP FESTIVE LIMITED EDITION

(2021) INDIA

→ Fido™ jumps in to celebrate the Indian festival Dussehra in this culturally relevant pack that brings the festivities' patterns, textiles, and music to life.

LAY'S HOT POT & EGG YOLK DEEP RIDGED

(2020) CHINA

→ Playful characters bring the fire with this flavor inspired by the beloved communal meal's hot, flavorful ingredients.

GATORADE
STAINLESS STEEL BOTTLE

(2020) **UNITED STATES**

→ Athlete collaboration fuels innovation, so we teamed up with professional players to design a stainless steel bottle that's as game-ready as they are.

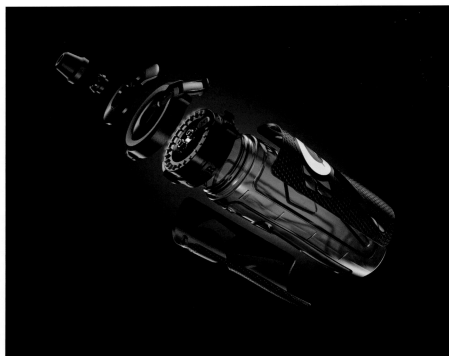

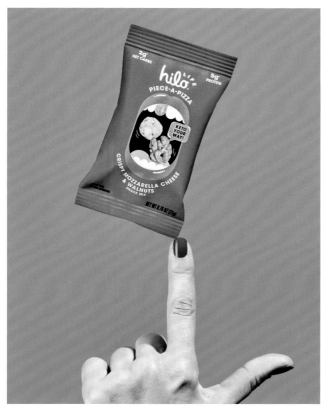

MTN DEW
DEWNITED (2019) UNITED STATES
CAMPAIGN

→ A limited edition series with fifty collectible, state-specific labels celebrates the flavors that unite us.

7UP LIMITED EDITION VINTAGE ART CAN SERIES

(2015) GLOBAL

→ These commemorative 7UP cans celebrate the original lemon-lime beverage with packaging spanning six decades of 7UP heritage for a look that's as fresh and enduring as ever.

OFF THE EATEN PATH

(2019) UNITED STATES

→ The on-the-go veggie snack was born out of an effort to discover new delicious and nutritious snacks, and its ingredient-driven visual identity invites people to do just that.

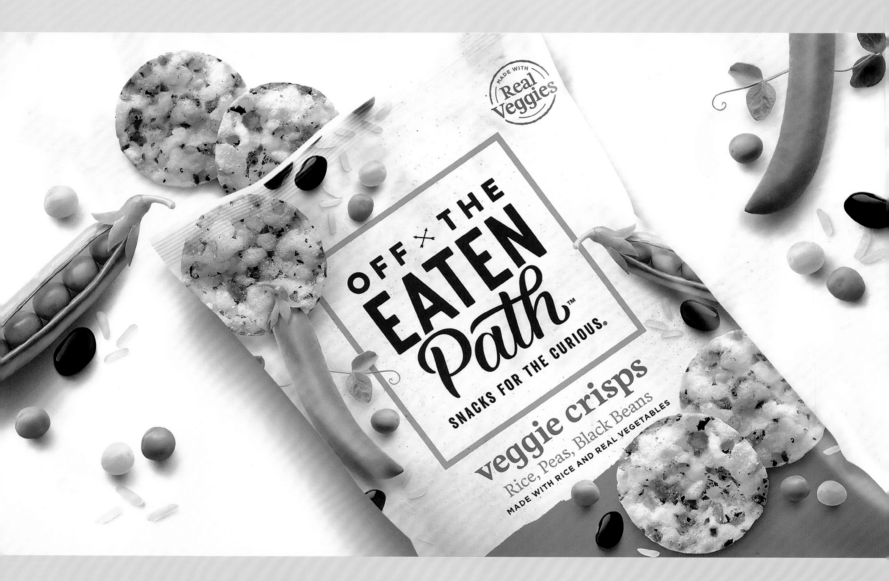

5g
Protein
PER SERVING

OFF × THE
EATEN
Path™

SNACKS FOR THE CURIOUS.

veggie puffs
Spicy Cheddar FLAVORED
MADE WITH REAL VEGETABLES

No
Artificial
COLORS
OR
FLAVORS

NON
GMO
Project
VERIFIED
nongmoproject.org

Net Wt. 4 ½ oz (126.57g)   VEGGIE SNACKS   ⓤ

MADE WITH
Real
Veggies

OFF × THE
EATEN
Path™

SNACKS FOR THE CURIOUS.

chickpea veggie crisps
Rice, Chickpeas, Peas, Black Beans
MADE WITH REAL PURPLE SWEET POTATOES

No
Artificial
PRESERVATIVES
OR
FLAVORS

NON
GMO
Project
VERIFIED
nongmoproject.org

Net Wt. 6¼ oz (177.1g)   VEGGIE & RICE CRISPS   ⓤ

SMARTFOOD PHOTOGRAPHY (2020) UNITED STATES

→ Lights, camera, action! Our new editorial lens sets the tone for the future of Smartfood.

LIFEWTR
LAUNCH

(2017) GLOBAL

→ Our premium water brand makes an entrance with a limited edition chiller designed by Studio Job.

As part of a PepsiCo exhibit during Milan Design Week, the biggest annual design event in the world, we commissioned a group of design visionaries to reinterpret people's experiences with a series of our iconic brands.

LIFEWTR
SERIES N°12—
TRUE COLORS

(2021) UNITED STATES

→ The series inspires everyone to get out and do what they
love through colorful artwork that embraces individuality
and self-expression.

LEMON LEMON
VISUAL IDENTITY 2017 UNITED STATES

→ Playful, sunny vibes and vintage-inspired illustrations invite you
to feel the fizz and get away.

7UP✕ONLY

→ Our collaboration with the international
fashion brand brings nostalgic iconography
and logos together for a collection of
vintage-inspired pieces.

324

LIFEWTR PAPER BOTTLE

(2020) UNITED STATES

→ Through developing and scaling the world's first 100% recyclable paper bottle, we're showcasing the power of human-centered design to reinvent packaging materials.

AQUAFINA
VISUAL IDENTITY

(2020) GLOBAL

→ The visual refresh focuses on the
essentials to create a look that's simple,
clean, and pure, just like Aquafina.

7UP (2021) VIETNAM
SUMMER
VIETNAM

→ Vietnam's natural beauty and iconic beaches are front and center on these limited edition cans that invite you to relax and enjoy each summery sip.

7UP FIDO DIDO HOUSE

(2019) EUROPE

→ An immersive installation in London's Covent Garden celebrates the return of '90s icon Fido Dido and invites people to find their chill.

FIDO DIDO

LANGLEY STREET

WELCOME

PEPSI
PERFECT (2015) UNITED STATES

→ To usher in October 21, 2015, a date made famous by one of the most beloved and futuristic film trilogies, a once-in-a-lifetime product merges real life with science fiction.

INNOVATION IS
ALL ABOUT LOOKING
AT WHAT EVERYBODY
ELSE LOOKS AT AND SEEING
OPPORTUNITIES THAT
NOBODY ELSE SEES. THAT'S
WHY **DIVERSITY** IS
INTEGRAL TO
EVERY DESIGN-DRIVEN
CULTURE.

WILD
EASY

MADE WITH REAL JUICE

NEON ZEBRA

(2021) UNITED STATES

→ Design-led innovation paves the way for us to shake things up with a line of wildly easy-to-use non-alcoholic cocktail mixers.

PEPSI NFL
LIMITED EDITION

(2020) MEXICO

→ A collection of cans celebrating Mexico's most beloved football teams kicks off the season.

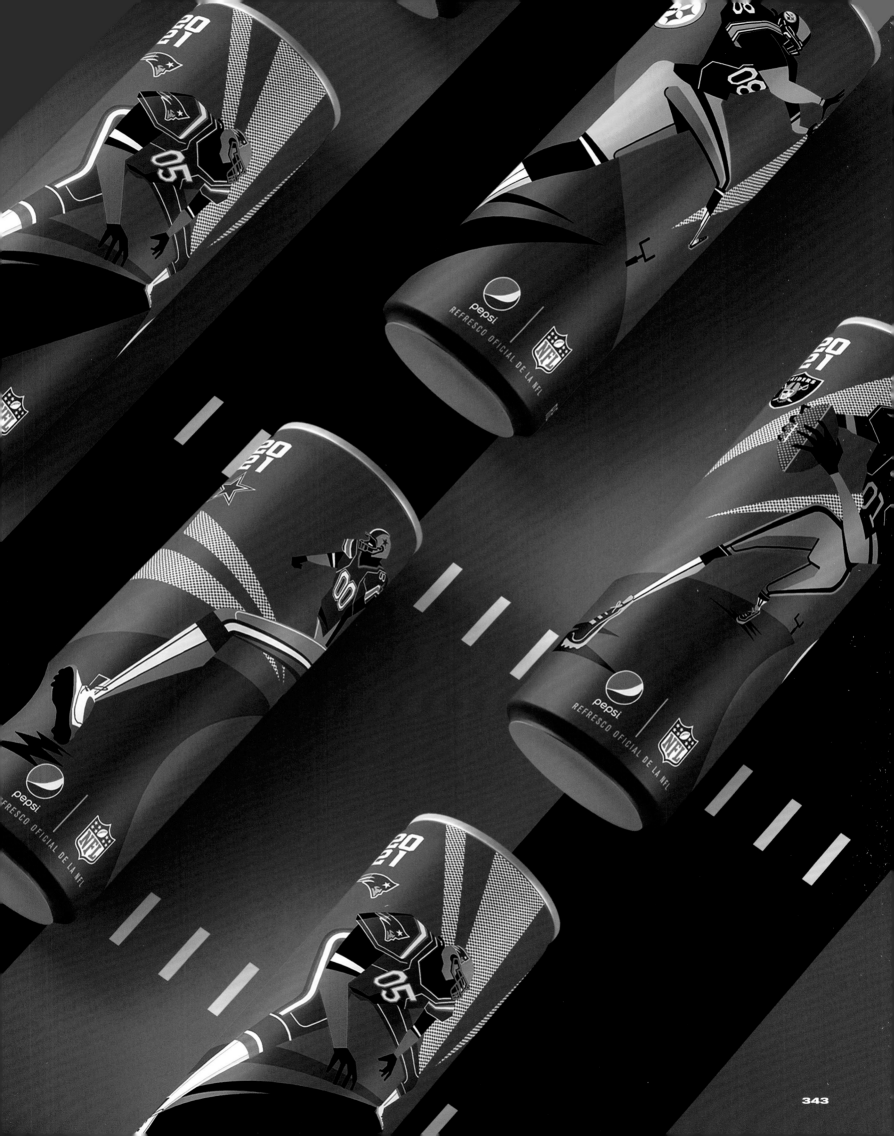

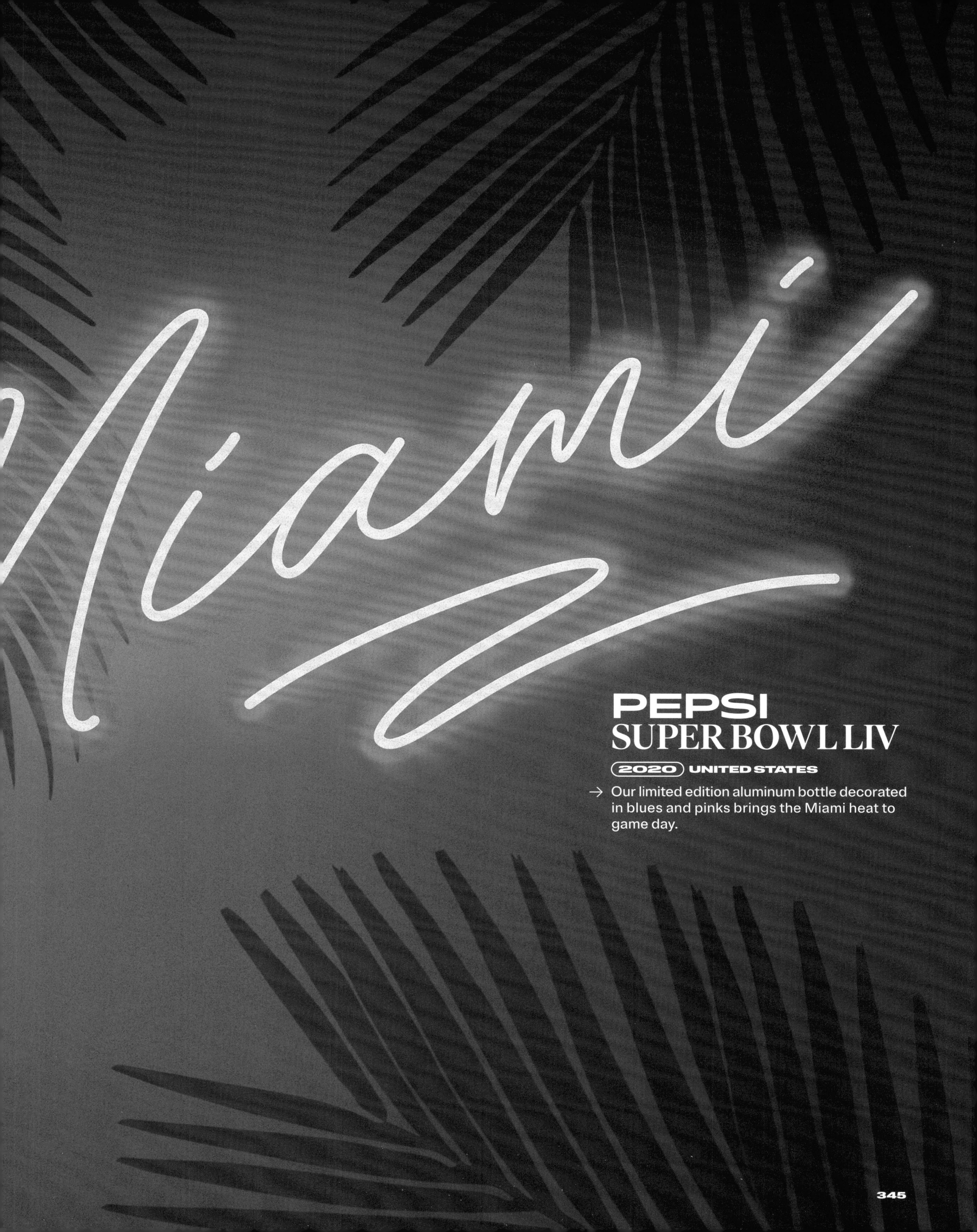

Miami

PEPSI
SUPER BOWL LIV

(**2020**) UNITED STATES

→ Our limited edition aluminum bottle decorated in blues and pinks brings the Miami heat to game day.

RUFFLES
✕ NBA

→ Limited edition packs and merch put
the ball in your court.

PEPSI SB LIII
LACES CAN

(2019) UNITED STATES

→ A limited edition collection of texturized, football-inspired cans is a winning touchdown.

PEPSI × FOOTBALL

→ The colors of different countries'
flags blend with our favorite shade of
blue for an illustrated celebration of
how the biggest fans in sports come
together when they cheer.

MTN DEW
VOO—DEW

(2020) UNITED STATES

→ The chilling return of a thrilling mystery
flavor keeps you guessing with hidden clues
and haunting illustrations that capture the
Halloween spirit.

MTN DEW × FILA
2017 SOUTH KOREA
→ An irreverent matchup makes for a high-
energy streetwear collection reflective of
our brand's signature attitude.

MTN DEW
BAJA BLAST

(2021) UNITED STATES

→ The flavor-forward world bursts with unique illustrations and characters to transport Dew Nation to Baja Island, a mythic, tropical locale where land and sea collide.

WE ARE THE AMBASSADOR OF A HUMAN-CENTERED APPROACH TO **BUSINESS, INNOVATION,** AND **LIFE.**

PEPSI
CHALLENGERS

(2022) MEXICO

→ Our team in Latin America reps all things Pepsi with these limited edition letterman jackets designed just for them.

PEPSI
PA'L NORTE

(**2022**) **MEXICO**

→ A commemorative can for Mexico's biggest
musical event puts the festival's iconic lion
mascot center stage.

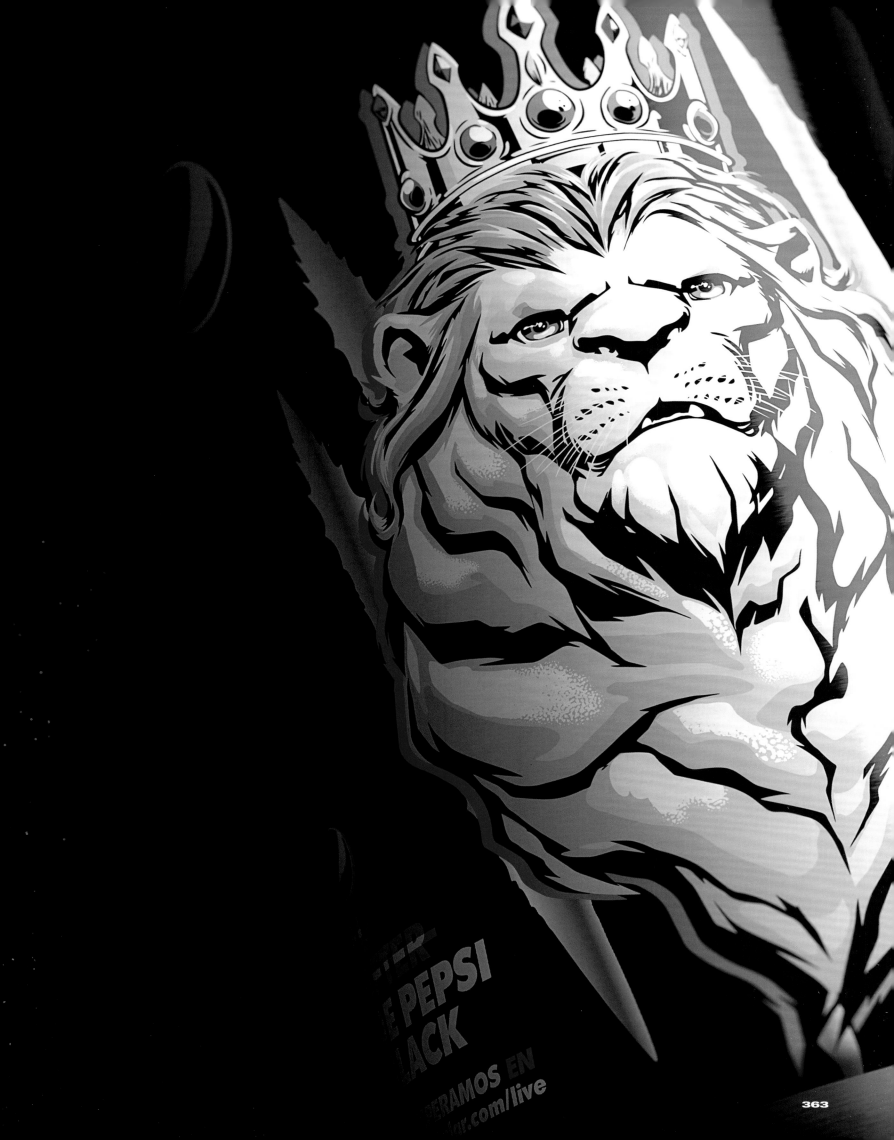

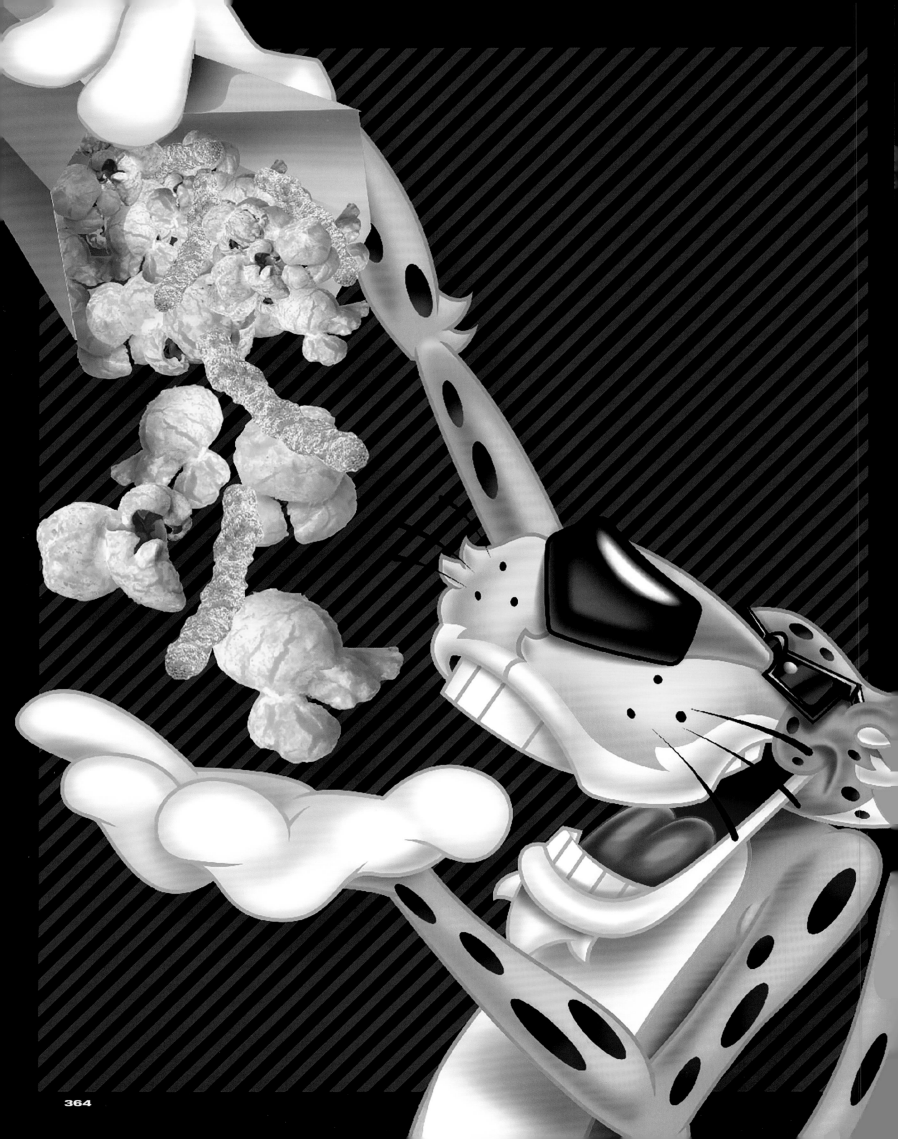

CHEETOS
POPCORN MIX (2019) UNITED STATES

→ A poppin' combo brings even more boldness and
fun to our favorite spokescheetah's brand.

RUFFLES✕NBA
ALL-STAR BAGS

(2022) UNITED STATES

→ Bold colors, patterns, and photographs of some of our favorite players make 500 limited edition bags must-have collectibles.

CHEETOS POPCORN RETAIL

(2020) UNITED STATES

→ Our spokescheetah Chester is always extra,
so we took things up a notch to introduce
Cheetos Popcorn.

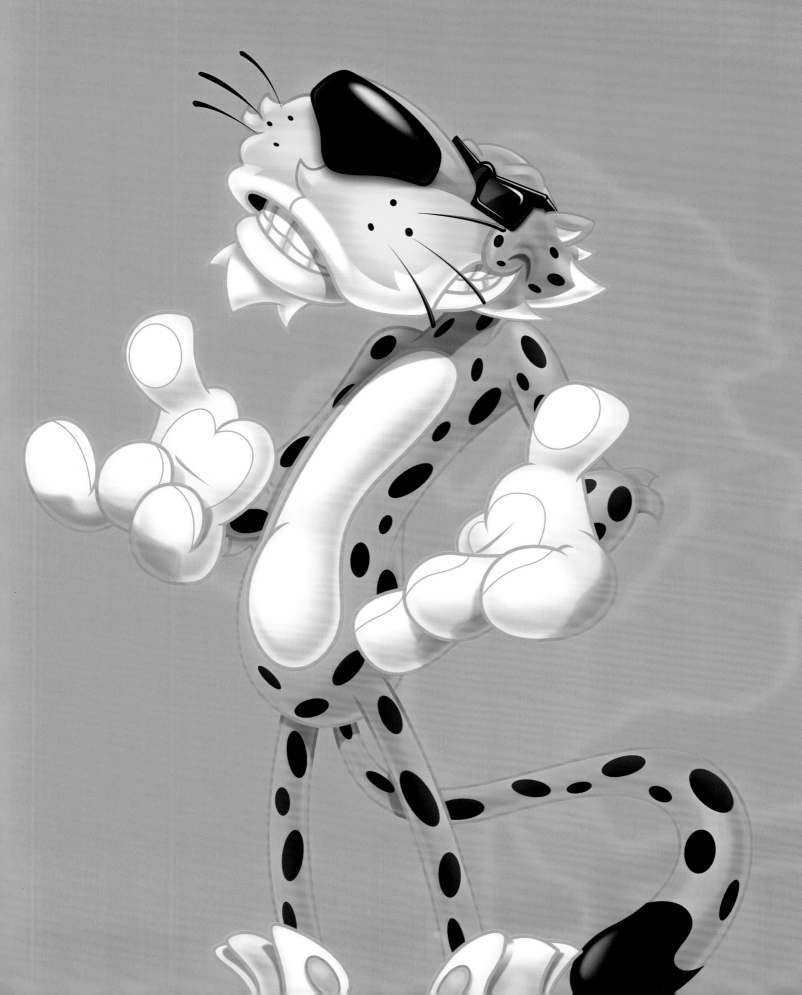

GATORADE
FUEL LAB

(2016) UNITED STATES

→ Our interactive showcase at one of the biggest innovation festivals in Austin introduces Gx, an ecosystem of science-backed hydration solutions, to the world.

LAY'S SUMMER CAMPAIGN

(2020) CHINA

→ Smile packs with playful personalities introduce fan-favorite flavors like Beijing Duck and White Rabbit Candy.

PEPSI BAHIA
LIMITED EDITION

(2021) BRAZIL

→ Thematic virtual cans celebrate Bahia's independence and irreverent energy with depictions of the Brazilian state's iconic architecture, food, and culture.

BUBLY PRIDE

→ Our rainbow-colored cans bring a smile
to everyone's face.

USA
ARRIVAL
08 MAY 2011
GERMANY
UNITED STATES
CUSTOM

Taste of...
MEXICO
WAVY LIME & SEA SALT
FLAVORED

Lay's®

Potato Chips

Taste of...
Germany
Beer and Brats
FLAVORED

Lay's®

Potato Chips

ABCD
MEXICO
0123
26 AUG 2016
ARRIVED

LAY'S
FLAVOR TRIP

(2020) **UNITED STATES**

→ Nostalgic bags tap into vintage travel illustrations to ignite optimism and a sense of adventure with limited edition flavors inspired by four dream destinations.

PEPSI CHINESE NEW YEAR

(2020) CHINA

→ The Year of the Rat calls for a fresh and auspicious start with three bold characters that infuse each sip with a little luck.

PEPSI

新年快乐

百事可乐

可乐型汽水 净含量330毫升

PEPSI

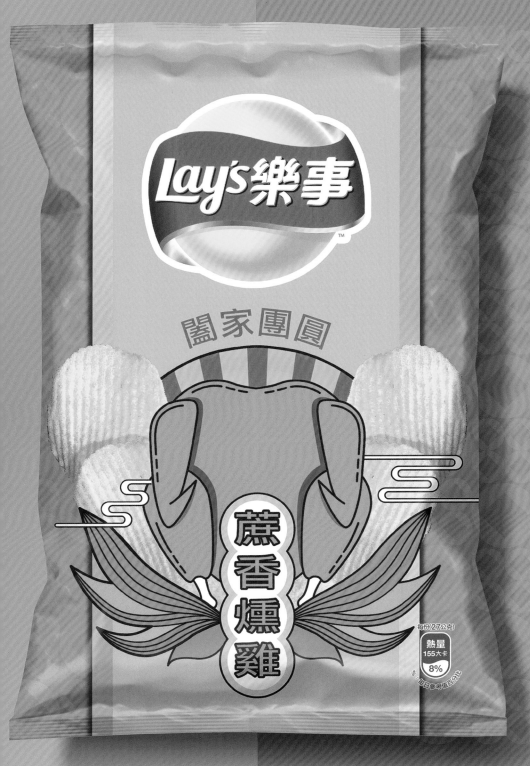

LAY'S CHINESE NEW YEAR LIMITED EDITION

(2020) CHINA

→ Modern touches and familiar traditions combine to welcome the Year of the Rat.

7UP CLEARLY CAMPAIGN

(2021) GLOBAL

→ With graphic illustrations grounded in the iconic images of 7UP, our forward-thinking take on the lemon-lime original serves up a fizzy, fresh world where Fido Dido can have even more fun.

SENSATIONS JUBILEE EDITION

(2022) WEST EUROPE

→ Regal flourishes are the crowning glory of these limited edition packs that let good taste reign to commemorate the Queen's Platinum Jubilee.

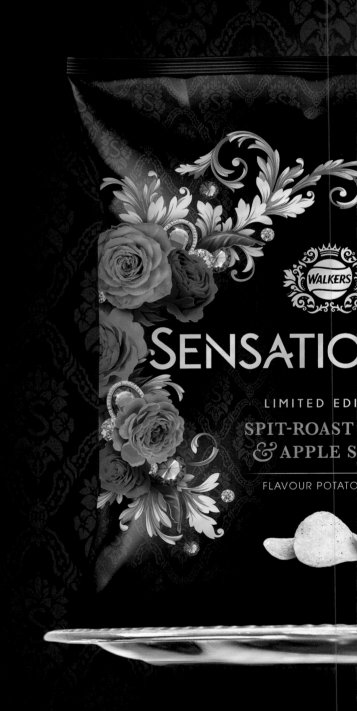

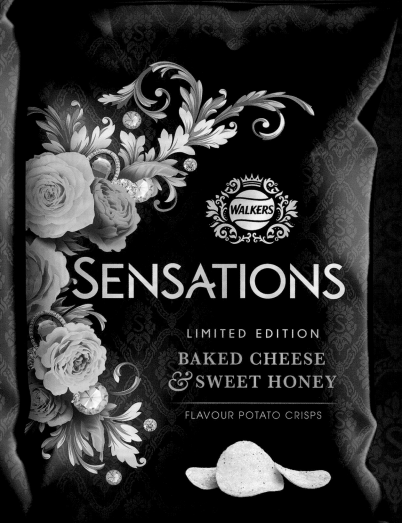

STACY'S
RISE PROJECT (2020) UNITED STATES

→ Each year, Stacy's stays true to its roots as a woman-founded brand and uplifts women entrepreneurs on and off the pack.

WE EMPLOY CURIOSITY, OPTIMISM, AND KINDNESS TO DRIVE GREAT INNOVATION AND GREAT BUSINESS.

BUBLY
LIFESTYLE VISUAL IDENTITY

(2021) UNITED STATES

→ A playful, bold, and flavor-forward visual identity
system brings personality and fun to the everyday.

MTN DEW
MAJOR MELON
(2020) **UNITED STATES**

→ The first new permanent MTN DEW
flavor in over a decade launches with
a fresh, fluorescent world.

MAJOR MELON™
CHANGING
AVOR
MAJOR MELON
DEW® Charged with Watermelon Flavor with Other Natural Flavors
MTN DEW
MAJOR MELON™
IS A WATERMELON
FLAVORED DEW®

MTN DEW GINGERBREAD SNAP'D

(2021) UNITED STATES

→ Cheeky illustrations tell the story of the gingerbread men who created this new flavor (and earned themselves a spot on the naughty list in the process).

LAY'S SMILE CAMPAIGN

(2016) CHINA

→ Smiles are contagious, and these must-share packs invite you to say "cheese" with playful and interactive illustrations.

CHEETOS
REDESIGN

(2020) MEXICO

→ A mischievous typographic logo revamps Cheetos Mexico and brings the Chester vibe to a new design system.

PEPSI
GLASS
BOTTLE

→ The single-serve glass bottle puts
a twist on our iconic cola brand.

PEPSI
GLASS TUMBLER
(2012) UNITED STATES

→ Our signature glass fuses an elevated, ergonomic design with a bold swirl to reflect the brand's youthful spirit.

PEPSI ✕
EXPO 2020 DUBAI

(2020) GLOBAL

→ Each can's AR feature unlocks to send fans on
fizzy, futuristic journeys around the world.

415

MTN DEW
GAMEFUEL×
DR DISRESPECT

2020 UNITED STATES

→ We teamed up with the well-known gaming streamer to create an epic visual identity that resonates in esports.

TOGETHER, MARKETING
AND DESIGN CAN CREATE
PURPOSE-DRIVEN BRANDS THAT
INSPIRE POSITIVE AND
LASTING CHANGE.

HUMAN-CENTERED
DESIGN IS THE HEART OF
PEPSICO, AND THE THOUGHTFUL,
CREATIVE APPROACH
DESIGN BRINGS TO EVERY PROJECT
HELPS OUR BRANDS REACH
AND CONNECT WITH BILLIONS
OF PEOPLE AROUND
THE WORLD EVERY DAY.

JANE WAKELY

→ EXECUTIVE VICE PRESIDENT, CHIEF CONSUMER
AND MARKETING OFFICER, AND CHIEF
GROWTH OFFICER, INTERNATIONAL FOODS

SENSATIONS
NAAN (2022) WEST EUROPE

→ An Indian taste fusion inspired an identity bursting with traditional patterns and mouthwatering flavor cues.

DORITOS RAINBOW SPECIAL EDITION

(2019) MEXICO

→ Through rainbow-emblazoned bags and multicolored chips, this technicolor identity celebrates Pride with an outpouring of love for the LGBTQ+ community.

DORITOS
BLAZIN' BUFFALO RANCH KITS

(2020) UNITED STATES

→ An influencer kit steeped in the legendary characters and timeless taste of the Wild West brings back Blazin' Buffalo Ranch Doritos to launch Flavor Drop Shop.

EARTHSHINE

2019 UNITED STATES

→ A lineup of customizable cold-brewed products
makes a splash with simple and modern lines
capturing the beauty of nature.

PEPSI✕GARAGE ITALIA CUSTOMS

2016 GLOBAL

→ An audaciously immersive collaboration kicks things into high gear.

LAY'S
UCL FINAL
ACTIVATION

(2019) GLOBAL

→ The engaging experience invites football
fans on an interactive flavor journey.

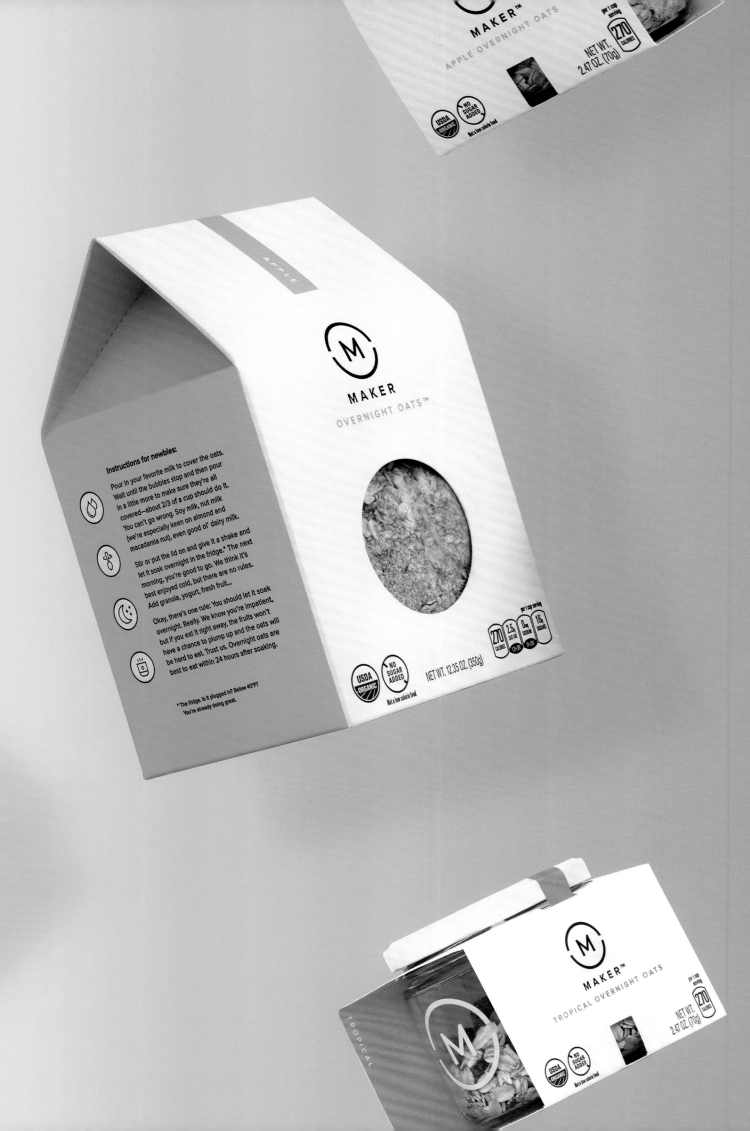

MAKER

OVERNIGHT OATS™

Instructions for newbies:

Pour in your favorite milk to cover the oats. Wait until the bubbles stop and then pour in a little more to make sure they're all covered—about 2/3 of a cup should do it. You can't go wrong. Soy milk, nut milk (we're especially keen on almond and macadamia nut), even good ol' dairy milk.

Stir or put the lid on and give it a shake and let it soak overnight in the fridge.* The next morning, you're good to go. We think it's best enjoyed cold, but there are no rules. Add granola, yogurt, fresh fruit...

Okay, there's one rule: You should let it soak overnight. Really. We know you're impatient, but if you eat it right away, the fruits won't have a chance to plump up and the oats will be hard to eat. Trust us. Overnight oats are best to eat within 24 hours after soaking,

*The fridge. Is it plugged in? Below 40°F? You're already doing great.

NET WT. 12.35 OZ. (350g)

APPLE

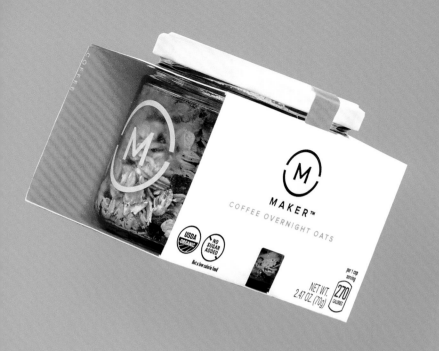

MAKER (2017) UNITED STATES
OVERNIGHT OATS

→ Our sleek, reusable kit makes these easy-to-prep, nutritious breakfasts clean and simple from the inside out.

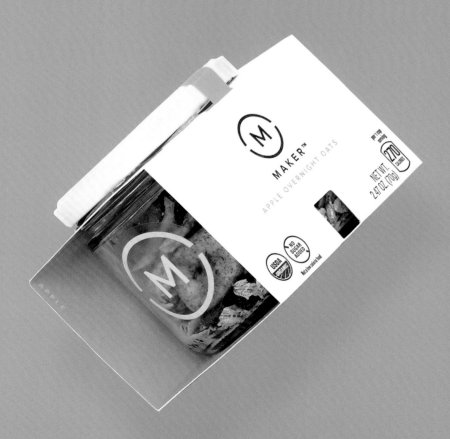

SLEEK
CAN REDESIGN

→ Everyone's favorite beverages get
the sleek can treatment.

WE LIKE TO TRANSFORM PROBLEMS INTO OPPORTUNITIES—WE SEE **POTENTIAL** WHERE OTHERS SEE CHALLENGES.

LAY'S GLOBAL PACKAGING

(2019) GLOBAL

→ A modern redesign of the world's biggest snack brand makes history by uniting over 300 global flavors with a fresh brand identity.

Sabritas®

Adobadas

papas fritas
sabor adobo **CONT. NET. 42 g**

Este envase aporta:

Grasa Saturada 57 Cal	Otras Grasas 63 Cal	Azúcares Totales 0 Cal	Sodio 196 mg	Energía 215 Cal
28%	16%	0%	10%	

% de los nutrimentos diarios

Potato Chips

黄瓜
Cucumbe

Sabritas®

Crema y
Especias

papas fritas
con sabor
crema y especias **CONT. NET. 42 g**

Este envase aporta:

Grasa Saturada 57 Cal	Otras Grasas 63 Cal	Azúcares Totales 0 Cal	Sodio 196 mg	Energía 215 Cal
28%	16%	0%	10%	

% de los nutrimentos diarios

Lay's®

Yoğurt ve Mevsim
Yeşillikli

PEPSI-COLA
SODA SHOP

2021 UNITED STATES

→ Our beloved Pepsi heritage logo is the cherry on top of this fun and modern twist on nostalgia.

SODA SHOP

CREAM SODA COLA

FLAVOR WITH OTHER NATURAL AND ARTIFICAL FLAVORS

MTN DEW
SPARK

(2020) UNITED STATES

→ To introduce this new beverage exclusively available at Speedway, we created a visual identity that fuses the exhilarating raspberry lemonade flavor with the brand's signature attitude.

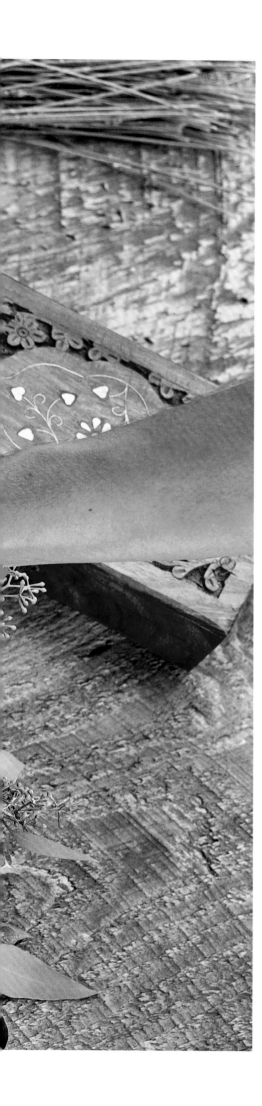

STUBBORN

(2020) UNITED STATES

→ Category-disrupting style, bold typography, and vibrant colors highlight these natural and unexpected flavor combinations.

QUAKER
COLLAGEN
GRANOLA

(2020) CHINA

→ A crisp look inspired by the pure simplicity of its ingredients makes every morning a good one.

TO BE A DESIGNER IS NOT
JUST A JOB. TO BE A DESIGNER IS
WHO YOU ARE, WHAT YOU DO,
AND HOW YOU FEEL. IT'S
A MINDSET AND A LIFESTYLE.

IT'S THE WAY YOU EXPERIENCE
THE ENTIRE UNIVERSE.
DESIGNERS ARE PEOPLE IN LOVE
WITH PEOPLE: THEIR
MISSION IN LIFE IS TO DESIGN
HUMAN VALUE, AND
WHILE DOING SO, THEY CREATE
BUSINESS VALUE, TOO.

MAURO PORCINI

→ SENIOR VICE PRESIDENT AND CHIEF DESIGN OFFICER

KOLA HOUSE

→ Inspired by the kola nut, the experiential lounge and event space offers craft cocktails and an artisanal menu.

SOULBOOST

(2021) UNITED STATES

→ Our sparkling water beverage featuring functional ingredients and buoyant visuals helps you feel the moment.

HELLMANN'S RUFFLES

→ A neon green palette and mouthwatering swirls bring all the creamy crunchiness of Hellmann's Ruffles to the surface.

QUAKER
GRANOLA

→ Good-for-you flavor is at the forefront
of this crisp, contemporary visual identity.

QUAKER
SMART CALORIES
BUBBLE MILK TEA FLAVOR SERIES

(2021) CHINA

→ Vibrant representations of our new flavors
and future-forward typography reflect
the balanced nutrition of this simple pack
loved by those on the go.

CHEETOS✕RIVA FASHION

Gx SWEAT PATCH

(2020) **UNITED STATES**

→ Our breakthrough innovation enables athletes to measure their sweat profiles, understand their unique hydration needs, and customize their drinks with formula pods.

INDEX

PEPSICO DESIGN

design.pepsico.com
Instagram: @PepsiCo_Design

——

First published in the United States of America in 2023 by
RIZZOLI INTERNATIONAL PUBLICATIONS, INC.

300 PARK AVENUE SOUTH
NEW YORK, NY 10010
www.rizzoliusa.com

——

FOR **RIZZOLI INTERNATIONAL PUBLICATIONS, INC.**

PUBLISHER: **CHARLES MIERS**
ASSOCIATE PUBLISHER: **JAMES MUSCHETT**
MANAGING EDITOR: **LYNN SCRABIS**
EDITOR: **ELIZABETH SMITH**

FOR **PEPSICO**

This 10th Anniversary Book celebrates a selection of
PepsiCo Design+Innovation projects developed by its
global in-house team.

BOOK DESIGN: **JD&Co. Design**
PROJECT MANAGER: **FAITH COHEN**
WRITERS: **RAMON LAGUARTA, JACOB LIEBERMAN,
SCARLETT MCCARTHY, MAURO PORCINI**
EDITOR: **SCARLETT MCCARTHY**

Quotes and texts provided by Mauro Porcini appear on the silver
pages throughout the book. They have been adapted from content
originally created by Mauro Porcini.

Quotes provided by the PepsiCo Executive team appear on
the gold pages throughout the book.

——

PRINTED IN ITALY

2023 2024 2025 2026 / 10 9 8 7 6 5 4 3 2 1

ISBN: **9-780-8478-7344-9**

LIBRARY OF CONGRESS CONTROL NUMBER: **2023931009**

VISIT US ONLINE

Facebook.com/RizzoliNewYork
Twitter: @Rizzoli_Books
Instagram.com/RizzoliBooks
Pinterest.com/RizzoliBooks
Youtube.com/user/RizzoliNY
Issuu.com/Rizzoli